GLORIOUS
AWAKENINGS

Lancashire born and bred, Clive Price is a freelance journalist and editorial consultant to Christian publishers, charities and church networks. He has contributed to a number of magazines and newspapers – including *Christianity*, *Youthwork*, *New Christian Herald*, *Renewal*, *Missionary Herald* and *The CARE Magazine*.

A past editor of *Parentwise* (*Christian Family*) magazine, he is consultant editor of *Compass*, the magazine distributed across the Pioneer and Ground Level networks of New Churches, editor of *The Christian Holiday Guide*, and UK correspondent for the US-based *Charisma* magazine. He provides editorial support for the King's Church network in the Thames Valley.

Clive has a deep interest in Celtic Christianity and is a frequent visitor to Ireland. He writes poetry, and contributed to Michele Guinness's anthology, *Made For Each Other*, also published by Triangle (1996). He is married with three children and lives in southern England. For relaxation, he plays the bodhran!

GLORIOUS
AWAKENINGS

Clive Price

TRIANGLE

First published in Great Britain in 1999
Triangle
Society for Promoting Christian Knowledge
Holy Trinity Church
Marylebone Road
London NW1 4DU

British Library Cataloguing-in-Publication Data

A catalogue record for this book is available from
the British Library

ISBN 0-281-05093-7

Typeset in Sabon by
Pioneer Associates, Perthshire
Printed in Great Britain by
Caledonian International Ltd

Contents

Contents

To God,
who gives me
life, love and laughs

Eleanor Mumford's talk about Toronto is on the
Holy Trinity Brompton tape 'The Coming of the Holy Spirit I', 29 May 1994.
Steve Hill's account of the Pensacola revival is taken from the
Brownsville Assembly of God video 'The Father's Day Outpouring'.
Lyrics from Iona's song 'Irish Day' are reproduced by kind
permission of Iona and SGO Music Publishing Ltd.

USEFUL CONTACTS
A factsheet of contact details of ministries and
magazines mentioned in this book can be obtained from:
'Glorious Awakenings', SPCK, Holy trinity Church, Marylebone Road,
London NW1 4DU.

Acknowledgements

Like award ceremonies, no book is complete without a few thank-yous! My wife, Janice, and our young warriors, Joshua, Emily and Jordan, have all been a vital help in keeping life, the universe and everything else in perspective.

Of course, this book could not have come together without the co-operation of all the good folk whose stories are featured. Their spiritual journeys have been a great inspiration to me, and to many others.

Those who have commissioned me to write over the years deserve a mention. In an indirect way, they helped me compile this book. How can I list them all? They include: Dave Roberts (former editor of *Alpha*), John Buckeridge (editor of *Youthwork*), Simon Jones (former editor of *Christianity*), Jill Worth (former editor of *Parentwise*), Billy Bruce (news editor of *Charisma*), Lee Grady (executive editor of *Charisma*), Colin Reeves, Brian Phillips, Peter Meadows, Malcolm Matson, Alex Noble, Wesley Richards, Gerald Coates, Laurence Singlehurst, Dave Markee and Stephen Strang. Please forgive me if I have left anyone out – next time round!

Where would I be without family and friends? So thanks to my sister Dawn, and my cheerleaders at Arun Community Church, Oasis Family Church and – in the distant past – Bethesda Chapel. A special nod to my stepfather, Bill, who gave me insights into Catholicism, a Welsh surname – and who paid for my journalism studies. I wouldn't have got this far without you and Mum, to whom we both owe so much.

1 *Strange signs*

Bodies strewn across the floor. Voices screaming like air-raid sirens. Anyone would think it was a battleground. The 'Toronto Blessing', which has triggered such bizarre phenomena since the mid-1990s, has certainly left some churches and Christian conferences looking like a war zone.

Uncontrollable weeping, shouting and roaring have been among other strange signs of this renewal movement, and it has blazed a trail indiscriminately across established denominations and 'new church' networks. From historic Anglican churches to young charismatic congregations, the Toronto experience has made its mark. And in many places the resulting response from the observers on the sidelines has echoed the cry of the ancient Jews when they were first confronted with the disturbing dynamism of Pentecost – 'What does this mean?' (Acts 2.12).

In a desperate bid to analyse just what was happening, there was a rush of reports. Some were quick to point out that the renewal was similar to incidents that had occurred at various moments throughout church history. Others attempted to attack the movement as a devilish deception at worst, and a psychological trick at best.

But it all seemed like early days when many of those first books and articles were issued, for most of the churchmen and journalists were working in the dark. In terms of the scale and intensity of phenomena, they had never seen anything like it before.

I was among those journalists sent in to the fray. Reports had started coming through early in 1994 – mainly via secular media, who had sent their journalists to a building at Toronto airport. I was working in the London offices of a Christian magazine publisher, what was then known as Elm House Christian Communications; and as the faxes, press releases and daily newspaper cuttings rolled in, my colleagues and I were intrigued at the accounts of masses of people falling to the ground after being prayed for.

We had all heard of that particular phenomenon before, of course. But I never liked the phrase 'slain in the Spirit', which some people used to describe the experience. It just wasn't PC (polite charismatic)! And anyway, it was something that usually happened at a weird, way-out meeting led by an over-emotional evangelist intent on increasing his mailing list. At least, that's what we *used* to think. Now, though it was different. The sheer numbers of people falling over; the long periods of 'carpet time' they endured – those were the kind of clues that showed that this wave of revival fervour was not like the others.

Francis MacNutt – well respected for his writings on healing – had brought out a book about the 'falling over' experience some four years previously, called *Overcome by the Spirit*. Later, the same year that the Toronto church made the headlines – 1994 – the book was reprinted by the Surrey-based imprint Eagle – with a foreword by Bishop David Pytches of St Andrew's, Chorleywood. He pointed out how the renewal movement that kicked off at this charismatic church in Canada had spread to other denominations – Anglican, Presbyterian, Methodist, Baptist, Salvationist, Roman Catholic and Pentecostal. Whatever the brand name, the flavour was the same.

It all sparked much interest – and produced some entertaining comments in our editorial department. 'Have you fallen over yet?' became the key question of the moment! But other phenomena started hitting the headlines, too. While travelling home on the train one night, I was talking with my colleague Dave Roberts. At the time he was editing *Alpha* magazine – as well as doing a hundred other things. (Dave is the Christian publishing equivalent of a Swiss army knife.)

We used to talk a lot about the Toronto experience. I really enjoyed our chats, amid the stressed-out commuters and city-slickers with mobile phones. Among the controversial news Dave and I chatted about were the reports of meetings in Argentina. Apparently taxis had been lined up outside venues to take people home. Nothing unusual about that – except that the reason people had to take a cab was because they were too 'drunk in the Spirit' to drive. It seemed that being overcome by God could now cost you your driving licence! The symptoms matched those of seasoned alcoholics, but these Argentinians had been intoxicated by a different kind of drink.

Debate about the phenomena would rage among us – myself, Dave and another colleague, John Buckeridge, editor of *Youthwork* magazine. Was it renewal or revival? How would we analyse it in a considered, thoughtful way? Someone described the movement as 'times of refreshing'. That seemed to stick with the wider church scene. It summed things up, without saying, 'this is the big one'. We journalists really liked the stronger phrases, like 'prelude to revival'.

Revival became a key word; a revolution was happening within church culture. In previous years revival had been the sole concern of individual prayer groups, and that was about it. Occasionally – if you were lucky – a preacher may have blown the dust off a story from one of the great revivals of Wales or Scotland. Everyone would look impressed, and then the history book would be closed once more. But the fresh fervour since Toronto was making the whole subject urgent and interesting again.

I could remember praying for revival as a young Christian. I knew my own life still needed sorting out, but it seemed right to pray for the glory of God to fall on the Church once again. Some years later I started attending a charismatic church on the south coast of England, where I still worship.

A former member of our church was a big Welshman called William Powell. This powerful Pentecostal man must have been well into his eighties, and his legs weren't as sturdy as they used to be. So during our times of worship he would hang on to a rail along the wall, swinging his arm in time to the music. He had childhood memories of the tail-end of the Welsh revival.

When I was editor of the magazine *Christian Family*, my secretary, Joan Winrow, could recall being taken as a young girl to meetings led by the fiery preacher Smith Wigglesworth.

These people were among my main links to any great revivals of the past, but now, through my own research, I was going to meet personally some of the key players in this latest renewal movement that had rocked the Church on both sides of the Atlantic.

My journalistic training told me to be objective. Analytical. Professional. Don't get personally involved in the story. One newspaper editor once told me off for being too chatty with news contacts. 'Just play it straight,' he said, 'you're too warm with people.' But occasionally I would close my notebook and try to comfort the bereaved person I was interviewing; offer some sympathy to the family whose business had just gone up in smoke; or check up on the victim of a road accident to see if they were recovering OK. Deep inside, there was always a Clark Kent inside me trying to get out!

While reporting on one church leaders' conference in 1996, I felt strongly that I should put my notebook down and join in. In other words, I should cease being the cold journalist for a while and just enjoy the proceedings. So I did just that. There were certainly some dramatic goings-on, and there was a heartfelt cry for national revival among the 1,000 church leaders from Britain and beyond who were attending the three-day event in Norfolk called 'After the Rain'.

The sound was almost deafening. The crowd let out a roar when Canadian preacher John Arnott proclaimed, 'For the first time in my life I have something worth dying for. It's the presence and power of the Holy Spirit.' With arms outstretched, the delegates – from countries as diverse as England, Wales, South Africa, India, Indonesia and Colombia – agreed with the sentiments from the man whose church has spearheaded the highly controversial 'Toronto Blessing'.

'We want to see this nation and every nation collapsing under the mighty power of God!' John Arnott cried. He had summed up a common feeling at the conference, which was run by the Pioneer network of 'new churches' and filmed by a BBC crew for the *Arena* programme. Even when the cries petered out, there was a murmuring of praise and prayer throughout the crowd. Shaking, falling, tears and laughter – the much publicized phenomena of this growing spiritual movement – were also out in force.

Long prayer and 'ministry times' meant that most meetings overran, but no one seemed to mind. I tried to take part as best I could, and ended up praying with a group of leaders from my own church. Our church administrator, Jeremy Wong, prayed that I would know 'God's heartbeat'. His words touched me, and I wept. Immediately I felt I should pray with another friend who was with us, Mike Jones.

Mike is an accountant, and I prayed that as a man of figures and statistics – he would have a new realization of the great numbers of people who lacked any personal knowledge of a loving God. Mike broke down in tears; he was visibly consumed with compassion for the multitudes who do not know Christ. Mike told me afterwards how my prayer fitted in with his own thinking. He would often wonder what we could do to bring down the walls of church that prevented people from coming in and knowing God.

At one of the main conference sessions, an appeal was given for all Welsh church leaders to receive prayer. The aim was to stir up again that great nation's revival fervour. But all that stopped when soloist Nikki Rose sang in Welsh what is acknowledged as an anthem of that awakening – 'Here Is Love Vast As The Ocean'. She brought the house down and people were screaming and wailing in response.

In a keynote address, called 'Out of the Old and into the New', Pioneer team leader Gerald Coates painted the picture of a transformed Church – one that reaches out to communities through meetings in schools, universities, hospitals, old people's homes and prisons. 'It's a new beat that's going on in the Church,' said Coates, encouraging people to preach the gospel in a postmodern culture – a culture that has lost confidence in reason and rationality. Pioneer team member Roger Ellis gave a multimedia presentation on Celtic spirituality, sharing lessons for believers today.

Meeting the great variety of delegates at such events is just as rewarding as hearing the talks. There were more Christian 'celebrities' than bottles of tomato sauce on the dining tables! Revival chat was going on at mealtimes among such people as evangelist Ian Andrews and his wife Rosemary; former ANC activist Joseph Kobo, now leading a network of churches in South Africa; and Dave Markee, who used to play bass for Eric Clapton, and now spearheads a lively church in Croydon.

At various times since this Norfolk event I have followed a similar routine with my notebook. I have put it to one side so that I too can encounter something of God for myself. That is another effect the renewal has had on people – it has made us greedy for God. 'More, Lord!' has become the cry of the post-Toronto revivalist. So while I still look at conferences as objectively as possible, at some point I enter into the proceedings myself – and allow the fresh wind of God to blow through my life. I have seen my own faith renewed, and my appreciation increased of who God is and what he is capable of.

For the past couple of years I have been in a process of what some would call 'personal revival'. Whatever you call it, 'it' has brought me to the point where I have become convinced that something deep and powerful is happening among the people of these ancient islands. Wherever I've travelled, others seem to be saying the same thing.

I want to introduce you to some of those people. Their experiences of personal renewal may be controversial, even disturbing, but they have become more effective servants of God as a result. My stories all come from the charismatic wing of the Church – that's because most of my reporting activity has been focused there.

However, hunger for revival is something that unites us all. We can all respond by opening our arms to the Almighty, and saying, 'Don't pass me by, Lord. I want all of you, and I want you to have all of me.' For that is the kind of prayer that will change our lives. Only then can we change our churches and communities. Because to share the good news, we must *be* the good news. We must be revived. These are exciting, challenging and uncomfortable days. But amid the uncertainty of our times, the breath of God waits to put flesh on dry bones. Every one of us can journey into revival.

2   *Toronto take-off*

It was January 1994 and Randy Clark was getting ready to speak at a little-known church in a small insignificant building alongside Toronto airport. 'I was scared that nothing would happen if I went,' he said later, reflecting on that moment. He had no idea at the time, but what followed was to have a massive impact on the Christian Church across the globe:

The night before, a friend of mine who had been a Baptist most of his life called me. I'd known him for ten years, but we'd only communicate once or twice a year when he'd call me with a word from God. He said, 'I've got the second most clear word I've had for you in the ten years since I've known you.' I said, 'What is it?' He didn't know I was going 'on trial' the next day! He said, 'The Lord says, test me now, test me now, test me now. Do not be afraid. I will back you up. I want your eyes to be opened to see my resources for you in the heavenlies, just as Elijah prayed Gehazi's eyes would be opened. And do not become anxious – because when you become anxious, you can't hear me.' That prophetic word was the catalyst to release the anointing. The rest is history.

It was a cold Canadian winter, and at that time there was no insulation in the building used by Toronto Airport Christian Fellowship. Yet after Randy spoke there, people were lying out on the freezing floor, apparently enjoying a new experience of God. 'We didn't really know what was going on when it started,' said Randy. 'We were just asking God to move – and he was. We didn't have any anticipation or expectation of what God was going to do. And it wasn't for several weeks that it began to hit us what possibly might be happening.'

Randy had been booked for four nights. 'I was only going to speak twice, and I brought my associate to speak twice,' he recalled. 'But I didn't feel like I had any sermons worth giving – beyond my testimony. In fact, I ended up staying 42 of the next 60 days. But the way I stayed was, John [Arnott] said, "Will you stay three more days?"'

'So we were thinking, three days more – maybe this really will go on for another three days!' But at the end of that time, they were asked to stay *another* three days – and then that grew to a week. They then started to plan a month in advance. 'It just kept growing,' Randy recalled. 'Then John began to say, "What if this went on for three months?"'

'No one was thinking three years – or even a year. It wasn't like immediately we understood the significance of what was happening. We were just enjoying what God was doing. We were so excited, we couldn't go to sleep. John was calling everybody he knew to tell them, "God has come! God has come!"'

Randy comes from the American midwest. Having grown up in a Baptist background, he studied religion at a Baptist college, and then went on to a Southern Baptist seminary in Kentucky. Later he became part of John Wimber's Vineyard movement, an international network of charismatic churches. Randy started a new church at the predominantly Roman Catholic city of St Louis in 1986, and was still based there in the summer of 1997 – the time he told me of his own journey into revival:

In 1984 I had been impacted by the Spirit, and for two years there were just major things happening – of healing, deliverances, of people being 'slain in the Spirit' or 'arrested in the Spirit' – whichever term you like best. From '86 it continued – when I started the church at St Louis – but it wasn't as strong. And from '87 to '93 it was just like everything dried up. It was very hard, no one was getting healed to speak of. There were only perhaps two or three terminally ill people healed during that whole period of time. It was much harder. I got disillusioned, discouraged, depressed. I was on the verge of a nervous breakdown.

Randy then heard about Rodney Howard-Browne, the South African revivalist associated with the so-called 'holy laughter' phenomenon. He attended some meetings led by the controversial preacher and received prayer, 'four or five times'. Up to that point, 'burn-out' had been affecting Randy so badly that he would start shaking if anyone gave him a stern look. Yet all that stopped when he was prayed for. 'I was touched, and I came back and I wasn't shaking any more. I was really restored in that area. The peace of God came on me.'

Something had changed in his ministry, too. 'I went to do a regional meeting for the Vineyard in the midwest and spoke one night. God came. Everybody we prayed for just ended up on the floor. People got healed. There was a lot of laughter. It was almost like a drunken party – in the sense of behaviour, laughing and giddiness, and some people not being able to stand up.' It was as a result of that meeting that Randy was invited to Toronto.

By now, the Christian world was divided about the new movement. But it seemed that for every church leader who objected to the strange 'manifestations' of falling over, laughing, weeping – and particularly the so-called 'animal noises' – there were many more reporters from the secular media lapping it up and filling their columns with dramatic stories of the 'Toronto Blessing' – the phrase first coined by a British journalist. Suddenly the daily papers had become interested in covering the Church again.

Unsuspecting journalists became directly affected by the renewal. One reporter from the *Evening Standard* newspaper fell to the floor after receiving prayer from John and Carol Arnott at a conference in southern England. Among Randy Clark's favourite moments is when God 'turned up' at a local Christian radio station in Florida where Randy was a guest. 'In your lifetime there are certain days you never forget,' he said, 'and this was one of them.'

It was January 1995. Initially Randy did not want to go. Lack of sleep was catching up on him. Exhausted and tired of doing interviews, he would rather have crashed out in a quiet corner somewhere. And as if to add insult to injury, it was an early morning programme – and the radio station was an hour's drive away!

'I tried talking the guy out of it,' Randy recalled, 'but he said, "No, you're supposed to come." So I went.' It was scheduled as a half-hour interview; and because he was viewed as controversial subject matter, Randy was questioned by the radio station's general manager: 'As we began to do the interview, the Spirit fell on the dee-jay – and he was trembling under the power of God. I could see this, but he had no idea what was going on.'

There was a commercial break after the first 15 minutes, when Randy told the crew what was happening. 'You don't realize it, but the Spirit of God is all over your dee-jay,' he explained. 'Why don't we pray for him right now?' The man received prayer. He immediately collapsed in that tiny studio – fortunately there was a gap just big enough to take his body! 'He was shaking violently on the floor,' said Randy.

'The commercials were over, and so the general manager tried to conduct the live interview while his own dee-jay was shaking on the floor right in front of him! He couldn't do anything, and he ended up having to tell the listening audience what was going on. So they asked me if I would pray for people over the radio.'

So Randy began to pray on air. Later, stories came in as people appeared to have been affected by something more than radio waves. It seemed that some listeners had unwittingly tuned in – only to feel the impact of this unusual renewal experience. 'One guy was driving a Coca-Cola truck, but had to take it back to the dock. He was shaking so hard, he had to go home!'

Finally the moment came for Randy to leave the radio studio. It was then pointed out to him that it was customary for guests to pray for the staff. 'So they brought the secretaries in, and I prayed for them,' he said. Wherever there was enough space for people to fall, fall they did – until all the floor space had gone.

Much later, having left the building, Randy tuned in to the station. To his surprise, the stream of renewal was still flowing. 'These guys had never prayed for anybody who'd then fallen in the Spirit. After all, they weren't pastors – they were radio people. But they just felt led to go on the air, explain what had just happened and say that whoever was listening, to drop by at the station for prayer.'

The radio station was linked to a local Assemblies of God church, so their building was opened up for those who wanted prayer. It became filled to capacity. Hundreds more then turned up, so they rigged up a video relay and sound system outside. 'They went for eight and a half months, six nights a week. Many people were touched.'

Randy was describing those experiences many thousands of miles away from home, while sitting at a picnic table in a Berkshire garden. He had been leading a series of meetings at King's Church, Slough, and was now taking a break. So while he was in the English heartlands, what hopes did he have for Britain?

I think of Wales and I think of the great revival that happened there. And I think of Scotland, and some of the great revivals there – and of Wesley and Whitfield here in England, and Patrick of Ireland and how he was used to evangelize much of Europe. There's a great Christian heritage here. I don't believe God is a God of denominations. He doesn't say, 'I am the God of the Baptists, the Methodists, the Lutherans' – he says, 'I am the God of Abraham, Isaac and Jacob.' God is a God of Wesley, Whitfield, Patrick and Knox. So when I think of Great Britain, I pray, 'God, I believe you made a covenant with those people. And I ask you to remember their prayers because they cried out that you would revive this land.'

Randy believes revival could be even more explosive in the United Kingdom than in the United States – if only for the fact that these islands are so small and compact. A spiritual awakening could spread quickly and effectively from town to town. 'My heart tells me that what has happened with the Toronto movement was just the first stage – to wake the Church up. And there's much more that God wants to do.'

3 *London's burning*

Queues in Knightsbridge usually indicate there's a sale on at Harrod's. But this time, it was a church meeting across the road that was pulling in the crowds. What could best be described as a fresh wave of spiritual renewal broke out at Holy Trinity Brompton – or HTB, as it's usually known – in the summer of 1994.

Sunday services were packed out, and tickets had to be issued in a bid to get everyone in. Normally a quiet month for most churches, that particular August saw attendance boom. Hundreds waited in queues that stretched across the church car park. On one occasion, more than half the congregation claimed to be visitors. 'God, we believe, is refreshing his Church,' HTB vicar Sandy Millar told parishioners at the time. 'People are experiencing the love of God in new ways – and finding the acceptance of a loving, heavenly father.' Numbers remain high to this day.

There is no doubt that the Toronto experience has helped put HTB on the map, but you will get a mixed reaction from London Christians about the church. Their responses will vary from respect to disdain. Yet few can argue with the deep impact made on the Christian scene by HTB and the quietly spoken Scot who leads them.

A key influence on Sandy Millar's own spiritual journey was a friend called Annette – she's now his wife. Annette became a Christian during her first term at university. 'She lived for ten years the life of what she would call a conventional Christian,' said Sandy, who was working as a barrister at the time. 'Then she was filled with the Spirit. And the moment she was filled with the Spirit, she "took off".'

In 1966 Annette sent a postcard to everyone she knew. The invitation read: bring a Bible and a tennis racquet – and come and hear about Jesus Christ. 'I was one of those who got a postcard,' remembered Sandy, who considered it a kind gesture. 'I knew there was an agenda, but at 27 I was arrogant enough to think I could probably hold my own with all this lot.'

Annette booked the nearest and most convenient conference centre, which turned out to be the Slough Diocesan Centre. 'It doesn't sound very exciting,' said Sandy, 'but it was actually a beautiful Elizabethan manor. So we all stayed there – about 40 of us. And Annette and her mother did the cooking.' They repeated the event the following year: 'I gave my life to Christ that Saturday night,' Sandy told me.

Like many other people's experiences, Sandy's spiritual journey had been influenced by a number of factors. He was brought up in the north of Scotland amid the 'granite spirituality' of the Presbyterians. His father was in the army, which meant the family travelled around. Sandy attended school and university in England.

It was later, after having launched into his career as a barrister, that he became increasingly attracted to the person of Jesus. A stranger on a train had once confronted him about Christ. 'I then bought a modern translation of the New Testament, and I just read it. I fell in love with Jesus – I thought he was absolutely amazing.' Eventually, with the help of his wife-to-be, Sandy concluded that Christianity was true.

Other changes were happening. 'I'd always wanted to be a barrister since I was eight,' said Sandy, 'and I became increasingly surprised by the fact that I felt more and more drawn out of it. My wife tells me that the occasion that I proposed to her, I asked her if she would feel the same if I was to be ordained.'

Sandy felt he had been doing a valuable job in the legal profession. He was taking on criminal cases with the conviction that the work should be done 'fairly and well'. But often while waiting for his own cases to come up, he would watch sentences being given to young people who were caught up in a spiral of drug taking. His wasn't a protest against the legal system, but everything within him cried out, 'There must be a better way than this.' He felt the beginnings of a desire 'to work at the top of the cliff rather than at the bottom, if possible,' he said. 'So in the end it just became an issue of whether we were going to do that or not.'

Sandy was attending HTB when he decided to enter the Anglican ministry full time, but it never occurred to him that one day he would be part of the staff there. In fact, as he set off to study theology in Durham, he believed that that was the end of his links with HTB. 'I can still remember as we drove away, thinking, "That's it." I thought of the wildness of the north, and that we'd finished with London. I wasn't altogether sorry. I was excited.' Sandy enjoyed his time in Durham:

> I just loved that atmosphere – Oswald, Cuthbert, and Lindisfarne – and all of that. It's just so inspiring. I never understood how anybody could fail to see that the Church in every generation has been actually following the gifts and ministries of the Holy Spirit. Cuthbert was healing people and raising people from the dead. That's why they venerated his bones – because of what the Spirit of God did through him.

Sandy was ordained in 1976. The venue was HTB, and he joined their staff as a curate. The church still ran the 1662 Matins in all its glory – with robed choir and the whole range of accessories. In fact, they had had sung Matins every Sunday morning since 1827. As Sandy says, 'Not even

Hitler could stop us singing Matins at 11 o' clock on a Sunday morning with a robed choir!' But into the breach came this new curate asking, 'Do you think we might change things?'

He saw how younger people came into the grand setting of this respectable Anglican church, and left looking bemused by it all. So gradually HTB started to acknowledge the changing culture of the outside world and apply charismatic-style freedom to the worship.

Later, when Sandy preached enthusiastically about 'the ministry of all believers', the question of robes came up. And when the robes went, suddenly the church had 800 'new ministers' who 'felt released and ordained'.

It could be something in Sandy's Celtic blood that hungers for freedom, and for a less hierarchical form of leadership:

Those who've studied Celtic faith – and I haven't – point to a sort of freedom and desire for freshness and a lack of structure about it, which I've always identified with. I first saw it in California. But I didn't recognize it as being Celtic. The Presbyterian Church in many aspects has ceased to be Celtic, and has become much more structured. But I've always admired the spirituality of many Presbyterian ministers, because they have a serious-mindedness about them and a humble spirituality which I love. But the Celtic bit which I think I would still want to identify with is that sense of freedom.

Sandy discovered how the restless, wandering nature of Celtic spirituality flourishes in a missionary situation. The historic Roman style of church is more settled and organized. 'I was very struck by that,' said Sandy, 'because it's so obviously true. And we're now suffering from an over-structuredness. You're discouraged from poking your nose over your parish boundaries and all that sort of stuff.'

Not all of Sandy's Celtic wanderings have been successful, however. 'The only time I went to Iona for the peace and the quiet, about three and a half thousand other people went for the peace and the quiet as well! So I've never really quite experienced it as it was, you might say.'

It was in 1985 that Sandy became vicar at HTB. In the ensuing years, the ground-breaking Alpha – an introductory course to the Christian faith – continued to be developed.

Alpha had started as a light meal and discussion in a vicar's home in 1977. But when curate Nicky Gumbel took on the course in 1990, he switched the focus to those outside the Church. The results were dramatic, as many came to faith. Now a professionally produced and carefully marketed package, the course has boomed. It is estimated that by the year 2000, more people will have completed Alpha than those who currently go to church in the UK. It has stimulated faith among the unchurched – and given new dynamism to many existing Christians.

The course is based on the Bible and the three persons of the Trinity – Father, Son and Holy Spirit. A crucial element is the 'Weekend Away'. Sometimes the teaching can be incorporated into a single day, but a whole weekend allows for thorough teaching on the Holy Spirit, and gives people the chance to cement friendships, take a break away, and find time for counselling, prayer and worship. Seasoned church-goers claim to have been renewed in their spiritual experience. Healings and profound conversions are reported to have taken place.

The 'Blessing' hit the church in the spring of 1994. Nicky Gumbel accepted an invitation to hear Eleanor Mumford, the wife of a Vineyard church leader, speak about her visit to a church in Toronto. Word had spread that unusual things were happening there, and Eleanor spoke of her experiences. Strange phenomena broke out as she prayed for people.

Nicky returned to HTB. As he said the closing prayer at a staff business meeting, similar things happened there too.

One or two were shocked by what they saw, but still the wave started to sweep through the church. Eleanor Mumford was invited to speak at HTB's morning and evening services the following Sunday. On introducing her to the congregation, Sandy said, 'If God is doing something that's immensely exciting and thrilling, we need to know about it.'

Eleanor admitted she went to Toronto because she was spiritually bankrupt. It was clear that she had longed for something deeper. 'I saw the power of God poured out in incredible measure,' she explained. 'We saw everything – save only tongues of fire.' Unusual phenomena included falling over, laughing and weeping. She quoted past revivalist Jonathan Edwards on the subject: 'If we see even a small part of the love and the glory of Christ, a foretaste of heaven, is it any wonder that our bodily strength is diminished?'

Eleanor's talk had a significant impact on those at HTB that day. According to the church's newspaper, *Focus*, 'hundreds were powerfully touched by the Holy Spirit'. Convinced that God had only just started, people were expecting even greater things to come. 'If you press me,' Sandy said at the time, 'I believe that God intends to bring revival.'

Renewal then spread to churches across Britain of all denominations. Newspapers and radio stations carried the news, though not all reporting has been positive, even to this day. But the media coverage has drawn the thirsty to come and 'drink' at HTB.

They were heady days when the 'Blessing' first hit HTB. But amid the spiritual highs, Sandy Millar attempted to bring some spiritual stability, too – 'attending to the keel, as well as the sails', as he puts it. Perhaps one of the most helpful, down-to-earth contributions to the Toronto debate came from Sandy himself, whose church had stirred the *Guardian* to write headlines like, 'Toronto Blessing has believers fainting in the aisle'. Sandy said in HTB's own newspaper:

> Let's take care – but let's keep our foot on the accelerator and let's go for it. . . . But we must go on reading the Bible; we must go on meeting in small groups and praying together; we must go on interceding and upping the intercession; we must go on cleaning our teeth and doing all the things we normally do – shaving and washing and hanging in there while these exotic things go on all around us.

HTB wants to press on from renewal to revival. Church members constantly pray for it, and Sandy talks about it. But amid the revival fervour, he has also been encouraging people to be committed to building a church for the long haul. 'These people have a nine-to-five job or a seven-to-nine job, and they want to know how to get through the day, how to get through the week, how to bring up their children. It seems to me that that's well annotated in the Bible. Paul writes to the Thessalonians, work, you've got to work – if you won't work, don't eat. Life has to go on.' However, Sandy said, we're on 'very safe ground' to pray for revival:

> And the more people that are doing that – which is why it's so exciting, it seems to me – confirms to us, as it were, that that's what's on God's heart, because he's stirring up people to do it. They like doing it. We've had our fair shares of excitements, for which I'm deeply grateful. But at the same time we need to keep one foot on the ground. That's not to dampen anything that's happening at all. It is to say that the Christian life is designed to be lived.

He has noticed signs of change around London – particularly in the friendships among church leaders – a 'unanimity of the Spirit', as Sandy calls it:

I don't think any single denomination seriously thinks that they're going to achieve now what they hoped to achieve on their own – in so far as that, I believe that's true. I believe that's even true now for the Roman Catholics, and perhaps I should say it's especially true now for the Anglicans. I remember Gerald Coates saying to me years ago that the only difference between the house churches and the Anglicans is that the Anglicans are quietly arrogant and the house churches are noisily arrogant. That was his assessment of the situation. There was just enough truth in it to hurt!

For the future, HTB has been committed to setting up a central London venue – which became known as the 'Millennium Village' project – for Christians of all denominations:

Just beyond the end of your nose, you can see the possibilities if Christians in London could get together and say, 'This is what we want, we've had enough and we're not divided actually – we're totally united' – like in Seoul, Korea, where the government takes account of the fact there's a very high Christian population. If you look at the number of Christians, there's quite a lot of us. And I think what God is doing is bringing us together and that will involve humility – for the benefit of the kingdom.

The Millennium project is 'a dream for the broad Church at its best'. HTB has already seen how Alpha has transcended the time-worn denominational barriers, particularly with its success among Roman Catholics. And it now has a vision for uniting Christians on a scale 'that makes it possible to think about impacting London, and beyond to the rest of the nation, in this generation'.

Sandy Millar has shown that he is a man with dreams; and, like a skilled craftsman, he carefully and consistently works away until they start to take shape. The late John

Wimber – who was a major influence on the work and worship at HTB – once spoke encouragingly of the church and its leader:

> One of the reasons I come back again and again and again when you ask me, is because of this: it's happening here. You are winning the lost; you are planting churches; you are worshipping God; you are feeding the hungry; you are doing the works of the kingdom. God is calling you to shake this city, and if you shake London, you will shake most of the world.

John, who used to lead the worldwide Vineyard network of charismatic churches, believed God had 'uniquely positioned' HTB to have a considerable impact on the Anglican Church and other churches around the world. He paid tribute to Sandy as a man prepared to 'risk everything' to build a New Testament church. John concluded: 'I'm not trying to make a hero out of Sandy, but I am saying that, in spite of his lovely humility, he is a man of God who I highly respect. I'm committed to serving him because I believe left to his own doing, Sandy will mess London up! And it needs to be messed up, doesn't it?'

4 *Northern lights*

Close friends Ken Gott and Wesley Richards read about the London outpouring in the press. Ex-journalist Wesley, who now leads a network of churches in the Thames Valley and West London region, phoned Ken to talk about Holy Trinity Brompton. Ken, a former policeman turned Pentecostal pastor, left his church in the north-east of England for London the next day.

'If you were God, how would you start a mighty move of the Spirit?' Ken later asked his own church in Sunderland. 'A thunderbolt from heaven? A fireball? An angelic visitation? Or would you get a friend to make a phone call? That's just like God, isn't it!' So the two friends attended a service at HTB. 'We went in there and stood at the back,' Wesley Richards recalled, 'watching what was going on.' People were being prayed for by Bishop David Pytches, former minister at St Andrew's, Chorleywood.

One of Wesley's team suggested they ask the bishop to pray for them. David Pytches obliged. 'Lord, come and get him,' was his impromptu liturgy over Ken Gott! The rest, as they say, is history. Ken's personal life and public ministry were transformed. Wesley remembers it well:

The funniest thing I can remember, was Ken right under the christening font. He was laughing – and it wasn't polite laughter. What's happened since then has been phenomenal. This is a move of the Holy Spirit. God is saying, 'I want my Church – I am the leader of my Church'.

I believe he is honouring his purpose – and honouring the prayers of men and women of God.

It was as if Wesley – Team Leader at King's Church Slough, Windsor, Reading and Heathrow – had dropped a pebble in a pond. 'The ripples haven't stopped,' said Ken, who, with his wife Lois, is Executive Director of *Revival Now!* 'They've gone on and on. And the ripples from that pebble have gone all around the world.' Wesley Richards and Ken and Lois Gott have since taken the flame of renewal around the world, and quite separately have become in great demand as speakers at home and overseas.

'God has been speaking to Lois and myself about the need to press into God for everything he has,' Ken recently wrote in his own publication, *Revival Now!* 'to press in for our churches, our cities, the nations. When God sees a determined heart, he responds. Blind Bartimaeus shouted out and stopped Jesus in his tracks. We've got to do the same.'

After his initial renewal experience, Ken visited Toronto Airport Christian Fellowship. He met pastor John Arnott, and a special relationship began. Ken has since travelled to other nations, urging people to move from renewal and into revival.

Ken invited John Arnott and his wife Carol to speak at his third annual 'Catch the Fire' conference at the Northumbria Centre in the summer of 1996. At the front of the packed hall were boxes of tissues for those who were overcome by weeping, and piles of 'modesty blankets' to cover women's legs as they lay semi-conscious 'in the Spirit' on the floor. This was a crowd prepared for action.

In his strong Geordie accent, Ken announced there would be a time of praise and worship. On cue, the band launched into the song 'We Wanna See Jesus Lifted High'. The worship leader – which is what they usually call the music director in charismatic circles – spoke of a confidence that the Church would fill the earth with 'the knowledge of the glory of the Lord' – but only by letting God 'light the fire'. The event had hardly begun, yet worshippers were already shaking and shouting. Musicians and singers flinched with the 'Toronto twitch', as that particular reaction has been called.

It is quite a sight to behold. Many people would agree that, at the very least, the renewal movement has made Christian events much more interesting to watch! 'What's it like down there?' Ken shouted from the platform. 'It's good up here!' He recalled the first time he went to Toronto. He met John Arnott in a corridor of the church, after being introduced by magazine editor Dave Roberts. John said he wanted to pray for him. 'That meeting in a corridor in this tiny building at the end of a runway changed my life,' said Ken. He could hardly get the words out. Speechlessness is yet another sign of the renewal:

> I was never the same again. I came back and changed my church. The Holy Spirit ruined a perfectly good church! He devastated this Pentecostal preacher in his sharp suits and his ties. It changed this region as the renewal came to our church – and affected Europe and the world. I owe a lot to Jesus. I owe a lot to the Holy Spirit. And I owe a lot to John and Carol for being faithful.

There were a number of contributions from Australian guests – and most of them collapsed in a heap on the stage, just as they finished speaking. The common thread running through their messages was expectation for revival – on the scale of 'thousands and thousands of families' making a decision to commit themselves to Jesus Christ. One church leader's wife had a vision of a huge hole in the heavens above Sunderland. 'The power of God was in this hole,' she said, 'and the people were just being sucked into heaven for salvation.' Her husband also had some words to share: 'God wants to put a fight in the army, like they've never seen before. The Lord wants to bring a warrior spirit on his body.'

Ken couldn't resist a cue like that. Grabbing the microphone, he said, 'We call the warrior spirit forth right now!' It was a powerful signal. The effect was like taking a cork off a bottle. Instantly everyone shouted in response. The whole crowd belted out a war cry; it sounded like one loud roar. 'We're waging war in the heavenlies,' said Ken, 'we're taking back that which rightfully belongs to the Church. We're taking back what is rightfully ours. This conference is full of purpose. There's purpose in the very atmosphere.'

The air was charged with emotional energy. All of a sudden, men bolted out of their seats and started running round the perimeter of the hall. 'This is the year of the Olympics,' said Ken, almost acting as commentator for the strange sights and sounds around them. 'This is the year of the runners. But the Lord would say, "I have put my torch in the hand of my Holy Spirit, who is not walking or crawling, but right now is running. He runs to the north, to the south, to the east and to the west."'

Revival is spreading like never before, according to Ken. 'These are unprecedented days. These are the greatest days we could ever be alive.' Despite the sheer joy and immense entertainment value of such events, they're not running conferences for the sake of having 'glory times', as he put it. 'As I've been praying, I believe what God is saying right now is, revival now, not revival in ten years . . . I believe God is saying, revival now, revival right now. I believe he wants to move renewal into revival. He wants us to use the word revival when we've been using renewal.' That's since been reflected in the name of Ken's ministry. Before they were known as Sunderland Christian Centre. These days, they work under the banner of 'Revival Now'.

John the Baptist's radical ministry has been used to illustrate the nature of the renewal. John caused a big stir, but he wasn't the promised messiah. He prepared the way for the one who was coming. In a similar way, Ken believes the renewal points to something greater that is yet to come: 'God says, "Will you push through for revival?" Where renewal cost us, revival will cost us even more. But we're saying, "Yes, Lord, yes, Lord . . . We want to speak revival, read revival – we want to be obsessed with revival." What a marvellous obsession to have!'

Ken Gott and others like him have been labelled 'carriers' of this spiritual movement. Among this band of New Revivalists is another northerner, Stuart Bell, who leads New Life Christian Fellowship, Lincoln, and the Ground Level network of charismatic churches. 'We're in such special days, we don't want to miss anything,' he told a leaders' forum in 1996.

Brought up in the Methodist Church, Stuart played in a Christian rock band called The Advocates in the 1970s. They were part of a whole wave of groups and artistes who were using contemporary music to reach the young generation with the gospel. It was the British expression of the US-born 'Jesus Movement'. Though it is not usually classed as 'revival' in the strict sense of the term, that period of time saw many young people 'turn off' drugs, drink and promiscuity – and 'turn on' to Jesus.

More recently, Stuart was instrumental in another movement that saw churches in one region of America become 'refreshed' and 'renewed' in faith and unity. It was in December 1995 that he 'blew into town with a heavy duty anointing' – as Pennsylvania church leader Melinda Fish described it.

Melinda took up the story. Church work in that region had been blocked by a deep disunity that had been gnawing away at Christians for years. Melinda pointed out that there is a 'tremendous sense of competition' in America – and it extends to church life. 'Everyone has an independent spirit,' she said.

Stuart began his American ministry trip in a town called Bethlehem, and then moved on to Pittsburgh. But disunity was clearly evident in the atmosphere. 'The first night Stuart got there,' Melinda explained, 'we were in the hospitality room. You could feel the tension in the room. You could cut it with a knife.' Still, it seemed that many enjoyed the meeting, and the Toronto-style manifestations took place.

The next day, Stuart spoke at the Church of the Risen Saviour which is led by Melinda and her husband, Bill. 'Stuart got up, minding his own business, and talked,' she said. 'He talked about unity, and shared this incredible story about a woman in his congregation who'd been touched by the renewal.' The woman had been dramatically reconciled with Stuart and his family when a serious rift between them was resolved.

'All of a sudden – wham!' said Melinda. 'You could feel the presence of God come down in the room. It wasn't like other renewal stuff. You could feel God in the room. People were bawling. I'm not talking "sniff, sniff". I'm talking "boo-hoo"! It was as though the floor wasn't low enough. You felt, God's here, it's time to get a low profile – and keep it.'

The next morning, 'The Holy Spirit showed up again,' said Melinda. 'A lot of people didn't even know a thing about the renewal. But the same thing happened – people were down, they were crying. Stuart prayed for a bunch of people, and a bunch went down under the power.' Christians were embracing each other in a wave of reconciliation.

'Word was starting to get out, and people were showing up. I never saw God give favour to a single person like I saw God give favour to Stuart Bell for Pittsburgh – they were eating out of the palm of his hand. He could have stood there and read recipes – and people would have responded. We were all conscious of the fact that it was like the presence of the Lord was there. It was like a fog.'

There was about a week of meetings, but then the time came for Stuart to say goodbye. According to Melinda, people were actually crying when they heard he wasn't coming back the following day. They saw Stuart as being used by God in Pittsburgh – just as Randy Clark was used by God in Toronto. Another church leader, Joseph Garlington, encouraged Stuart to stay on.

Christmas provided a convenient break, then Stuart returned in January 1996 with some of his family. And despite blizzards, people still turned up for the meetings. 'The miracle was the outbreak of unity,' said Melinda. People also started praying for revival. Melinda went on to write a book about the renewal, called *The River Is Here* (Chosen Books), endorsed by the conservative evangelical writer Jim Packer. He described the 'Blessing' as 'an international phenomenon that is now too big to ignore'.

5 *Sunshine state*

'Holy Spirit falls in London'. The headline almost screamed out at him from the page. American evangelist Steve Hill was returning home from Russia in the summer of 1994 when he opened up his copy of *Time* magazine. There he came across a whole-page article that focused on dramatic spiritual renewal at an Anglican church in central London. He decided that the next time he went to Russia, he would go via England's capital city. It was in January 1995 that he made that detour.

'I remember I was taking a ferry boat across the English Channel,' he said. 'I was looking out the picture window and there was a beautiful rainbow, past the white cliffs of Dover. I saw that and I thought, "Man, that's gorgeous."' Then over the ship's sound system came the song 'Amazing Grace' – played on bagpipes. 'I have never heard anything so beautiful in all my life,' Steve recalled, 'it filled the whole boat up with the glory of the Lord. And I said, "God, what do you have planned for me?"'

After arriving in England, Steve went to stay with a couple who had been friends of his for many years. As soon as he got to their house, he asked where Holy Trinity Brompton was – the church where people were joining long queues just to get in. It turned out that the couple themselves attended HTB.

They gave Steve a pile of literature to read. 'I cried for the next three hours – as I read testimony after testimony of the power of God hitting people, coming down, people being filled with the Holy Spirit, people being delivered from

problems and habits, marriages being healed – incredible
wonders of the Lord.' Steve arranged to meet HTB's vicar,
Sandy Millar, at three o'clock the next day:

> I walked into his church, which is right next to Harrod's
> – the ritziest area of the city – and I stepped over 100
> bodies trying to get to the pastor. These were Englishmen
> – they don't do this. I'd been around falling to the ground
> before. Just because someone falls to the ground doesn't
> make them spiritual. But I had never seen the depth that
> was going on here. I went across and I walked up to
> Sandy. I looked at him and said, 'My name is Steve.' He
> said, 'Oh my, we had a three o'clock appointment – but
> look what happened.' I said, 'Sandy, you don't need to
> talk with me – pray for me, lay your hands on me.'

Sandy laid his hands on Steve's forehead:

> When he touched me, the power of God swept through
> my body. I fell to the ground. I don't ever do that – ever.
> For 20 minutes, 'rivers' were flowing through me. I've
> been filled with the Holy Ghost – I've seen everything a
> man can see in missions. I got up 20 minutes later, trans-
> formed! I was brand new. I wasn't living in sin, but little
> did I know how dry I was until God soaked me. You're
> talking about a 180-degree turn. I got up and I was like a
> kid at Toys-R-Us.

Later, after arriving back home in the States, Steve prayed
for members of his family. 'I touched my wife. She said
two words – "dear Jesus" – and hit the ground!' His seven-
year-old son Ryan entered the room. Steve asked if he could
pray for him too. Ryan agreed. 'I touched him. He went into
a trance. He got up and was changed. His attitude changed.
Suddenly he realized there was power in the name of Jesus –
like "Don't mess with Daddy's Jesus." It was beautiful!'

Steve preached at a church of 1,300 people. He asked how many people were hungry for a 'refreshing' from God, and 300 responded. 'The Holy Ghost fell,' he said. 'People were immediately filled with the Holy Ghost who'd been seeking him for years. People were healed just like that. People who'd been dealing with an inner turmoil about something that took place in their lives – how we counsel all the time – God was dealing with that issue in five minutes on the ground.'

When Steve had worked in Argentina – considered to be a major 'hotbed' of revival – he said he saw people fall by the thousands. 'But they would get back up,' he added. 'There are people in our meetings who go down, and while they're down they have a visitation from God. We're beginning to sound like the New Testament – with visions and dreams and signs and wonders.'

Steve was describing his HTB visit at a meeting in Brownsville Assembly of God, Pensacola, on Father's Day 1995. It is all recorded on video. His talk triggered what has become known as the 'Pensacola Outpouring', which has gathered momentum from that day. Brownsville has earned itself international recognition as a church in revival, drawing countless visitors to the 'sunshine state' of Florida each year.

In his typically humble fashion, to this day Sandy Millar underplays his part in having been a channel for Steve Hill to receive such a powerful anointing. 'The fact is, God does what he wants to do,' Sandy said more than two years later, 'and I think that dear man was so prepared and so hungry that if anyone had looked at him, he would've gone off and fire would have broken out – because that's what he came for. And that's what we need to be praying for, it seems to me, then God will do it – some way.'

But the story had spread about Steve Hill, and in at least one person's mind the Anglican vicar had a special touch.

This particular man came up to Sandy after an evening service and said, 'You prayed for Steve Hill – I want what Steve had.' Sandy's reply? 'So do I,' he said. 'We didn't get very far after that! But I certainly prayed for him.'

Whatever people think about Pensacola – and the church has drawn more than its fair share of controversy – it must be the first spiritual revival to make it into the pop charts. Bestselling artistes Joan Osborne and Sheryl Crow have both referred to it in their songs. Media giants like *Time* and CNN have covered the story.

More than one and a half million people have converged on Brownsville to warm themselves by the revival fires. Stirred by Steve Hill's powerful preaching, no fewer than 125,000 of them have made Christian commitments. Church workers, evangelists and Christian leaders across the UK have boarded planes to get a taste of Pensacola. They have wanted to see if this was the real thing. Was it really a church in revival?

James Sharp cannot remember how he first heard about Pensacola. It may even have reached him first as a rumour. Even so, if this was a church in revival, he decided it was worth checking out. While visiting contacts at New York in January 1997, James and Justin Blake – both leaders at Revelation Church on the south coast of England – travelled down to Florida to see the phenomenon for themselves.

'We were out there for just a few days. I was initially sceptical. I was having a look to see if it was just Bible belt stuff.' James did have problems accepting some of the cultural differences he found. 'The role of women is minimal,' he said, 'and it's very structured. But you cannot deny that God is breaking in – and many, many people are repenting and getting saved. It's remarkable to see that.'

Another thing that struck James was the different scale of things across the Atlantic. He was sitting next to a 'very short, very annoying Mexican' who kept saying 'Praise the

Lord' – 'at 200 decibels', said James. On asking him where he was from, they discovered he led a network of nearly 160 churches!

'The meeting started, with the worship just gently trickling on. Suddenly the song changed key, the drums came in, the lights went up, the choir stood up – and there was this great surge of energy.' It was smoothly orchestrated. But it also 'sent electricity across the auditorium', said James.

'I've been a Christian for 27 years and I've never seen energy in worship like that generated out there. I could remember many of the songs from my childhood. But people were bouncing up and down as if they were at a Sex Pistols gig! It was incredibly energetic – far more than I've seen anywhere else.' James found a great emphasis on holiness, prayer and discipline – 'which has impacted all of us who've gone out there'. He feels God spoke to him about what it means to be like Jesus.

'Holiness is initially a personal thing. But then it goes on to issues like – what about my community? What about the lost? I've come back from Pensacola feeling passionate about certain things – that weren't even preached about there.' He said everyone returns from Brownsville with the same kind of story. 'You just end up coming away, wanting to spend time with God,' he added. For James, the knock-on effects included sorting out areas of his life that needed attention. He spent time 'just getting to know God again'.

Pensacola ignited a fresh spiritual hunger within him. Issues of personal holiness developed into issues of global justice and mission. It led to a career change for James within the Revelation leadership. 'We need to release you,' he was told. 'I've seen something,' he said, 'and I know it can happen here.'

6 *Another drink*

A massive cultural revolution took place in the 1960s and 1970s that turned Britain on its head. Then it did the same in the United States. It was called Beatlemania. When the Beatles arrived on the scene, everything changed. The world would never be the same again.

The 'Fab Four' had a phenomenal impact. John, Paul, George and Ringo won many people's love, respect and admiration – initially with just a set of simple songs and some natural home-grown charisma. Their spectacular success transformed the pop culture and fashion scene in both Britain and the States. The Liverpool lads' popularity was so great that they only had to endorse a musical or fashion trend, a social cause or religious philosophy – and immediately it would gain credibility.

John Scotland grew up with the Beatles' music, but he wasn't exactly a follower. 'You have to understand that in Liverpool, people were offended by the Beatles because they were part of the landscape,' said John, 'and suddenly the band moved down to London. A lot of Liverpudlians felt hurt about that, that they'd lost their group to the world. So I really wasn't a Beatles fan.'

All that was to change – when it seemed John was about to link up with the Beatles myth yet again. It was to have a big impact on his life – giving him a new perspective on revival and the kind of influence the Church must have if it is to change society. In 1996 John was speaking at a church in Norway when a local businessman offered to treat him to some new clothes, as a gift for his ministry.

'I was walking through a park in Skien, south of Oslo, and there was a Salvation Army band playing. I went into town and stopped outside this shop. There were two Norwegian lads on a soapbox playing Beatles songs.' John immediately felt at home. Then he entered the shop. 'I wasn't used to people saying, "Pick anything you want off the rack." I didn't want to be too greedy. But this friend of mine said, "Go for it, John, get the best." He picked me this suit off the rack. It was a Beatles suit.'

Father of four John was due to take part in a conference in New York. En route he saw a television documentary about the history of pop music:

The presenter said that the Beatles changed the whole music scene. They broke through in an area and broke tradition. It was as if God was speaking to me through it all. He was showing me this renewal movement isn't just about the music – it's a whole new thing God's going to do in the church. It was never the same after the Beatles. You hear many pop singers now say they credit their success to the way the Beatles had broken through. They changed the culture.

On arriving at the church in New York, John discovered that the son of the pastor was a Beatles fan. John also felt God telling him to buy the two CD compilations of the Beatles' hits. So he did!

I was singing phrases like 'Strawberry Fields Forever'. I was at a breakfast and I cut a strawberry in half – and I noticed there was a heart shape on the strawberry inside. I started singing the song. And God showed me that Strawberry Fields was a Salvation Army orphanage – salvation, orphanage – that God is our father and that we were orphans and now he's taking us in. This new move of God is going to be the father heart of God to the fatherless – the orphans – of which we have an awful lot.

Another Beatles song that struck him in a new way was 'Eleanor Rigby' – which spoke of a priest writing sermons for an empty church, and the multitudes of lonely people in society. 'That's true. If you think about it, less than 4 per cent of the population go to church. People are writing sermons that no one will hear – 96 per cent do not hear the message.' John started using Beatles songs and lyrics in his preaching, as an opener to different issues about personal faith and renewal.

John then met an American speaker with a 'prophetic ministry' called Larry Randolph. 'Larry is a prophet who can virtually read your mail,' said John, 'he will tell you things only you will know. We were going for lunch, and he said, "John, I fixed on you a few times" – but he never told me what the prophecy was!

'All he said was "Paul McCartney". I was frustrated with him. I thought, thank you very much – you whet my appetite and you don't tell me what the prophecy is.' Yet John realized that with the Beatles suit he got from Norway, he was acting out a prophetic statement – even though he can't play an instrument!

'The television documentary that I saw said that one key thing about the Beatles was that their songs were very simple, and the reason they won the world was that they had a happy, carefree charisma. They weren't too heavy. That's where we've got to get to as Christians.'

John felt that part of the ministry God had given him was to break the 'intellectual, theological, 20-point seminar' approach to Christianity – and to get people back to the simplicities of faith. 'I went to a church and all I could say was A-B-C-D-E-F-G. The pastor said, "What does that mean, John?" I said, that means "Back to basics."' He told one meeting in New York, 'The trouble with Christians is that we've been listening to radio for too long – everything is words that we hear. Now we're seeing things. God is conveying his message through a living demonstration.'

John himself has been something of a 'living demonstration' since he first visited Toronto Airport Christian Fellowship – just after renewal broke out there in 1994. His life was turned upside down.

John's wife Jean took up the story. 'It was February 1994,' she said, 'when a friend of ours in Canada phoned up and said something was happening down in Toronto.' They already knew Toronto leaders Marc Dupont and John Arnott, as the Scotlands had lived in Canada for a time, so they decided to check it out.

'It was so radical at that time,' said Jean. 'We looked at the manifestations and thought, "We've cast these out of people." That's what it looked like. It looked demonic. That was our first impression.' Another thing that struck them was how the renewal meetings would continue into the early hours. 'I said I wanted to stay right till the end of one particular meeting,' said John. 'but the meeting was still going on and it was 12.30. We were wandering round, observing everything. We went into the bookshop and a lady was placing an order. They said it would be ready in two hours' time. It was just like nightshift really – like a 24-hour church.'

John managed to catch up with John Arnott. 'It was like he was mesmerized with all that was going on,' he said. John Arnott went to introduce him to his wife Carol – who has a reputation for praying for people without warning. She had hardly reached out to pray when John fell to the ground:

Bang! Down I went. I couldn't get up. I was on the floor and I saw these two guys coming towards me, twitching. And I said, Lord, I don't want what they've got – don't let them pray for me. But they did. I got up and was relieved I could walk. I made it home and got into bed. When I woke up the next morning, the Holy Spirit was at the bottom of my bed. He filled me – and I couldn't talk in English. I just kept speaking in tongues.

It was Good Friday, 1 April. John had woken up at about 6 a.m., with Jean asking him what had happened the night before. 'He went to lean over towards me and he kept speaking in tongues,' said Jean. 'Every time he looked at me he just spoke in tongues. This went on all day. At first we thought it was an April Fool's joke!' The Scotlands attended a Good Friday service – and John had to take a notepad with him. 'We hadn't seen some of these people for a while,' Jean recalled, 'so they kept on coming up to John and asking him questions. He had to keep on writing down on this pad – he just couldn't speak in English.'

Two men – 'dressed like cowboys', as John put it – prayed for him. 'They told him he had to intercede for the city,' Jean said of the content of their prayer. 'So he went upstairs to do just that. Afterwards he fell asleep. And when he woke up he could speak in English. So the Lord began to move on, really. Then we came home.' But they returned to Liverpool with 'an intense hunger – a real hunger to see God do something,' according to John. 'So we asked God to send a prophet to Liverpool. But prophets don't come to Liverpool – they usually avoid it.'

At the time the Scotlands were running a church in the city. It was frequently the target for robbers. Jean said, 'We'd been home for about two hours and the church secretary phoned up and said there'd been a break-in. While we were away the church had been broken into again. We were thinking, "Lord, just move us out – we want a prophetic word to go." We were so low on numbers, we thought, "Are we wasting our time here?"'

A pastor friend told them a meeting had been hastily arranged with a speaker from Texas called Bobby Connor. Despite such a disappointing homecoming, the Scotlands went along. 'At the end he said to us, "Come tomorrow night – I have a word for you",' said Jean. 'The first night it was people with lots of problems. The next night he said he wanted to give direction. So we went along the next night and he prophesied over us. He said there was an anointing coming to John. It was going to be explosive, to set the captives free. He said, "Don't let anyone steal your dreams."'

That November, John returned to Toronto for a prophetic conference led by Marc Dupont:

As I was walking through the door, Marc asked me to get up and give my testimony that first night. I was standing there in my usual attire – shirt, tie and suit – and I felt this big pear drop hit the top of my head and come down with a warm feeling.

God said to me, 'You're here, John, for ten days – enjoy yourself – what would you like?' I said, 'I'd like to get drunk, Lord. I've never been drunk. I don't know what it's like. I'd like to get drunk.' So then he told me, 'You see all the people with ministry team badges, they're bartenders. And they all serve different flavours of drink. To get drunk you must mix your drinks.' So I sat on the end of every row. And every time someone walked past with a dayglo badge on, I reached out and took a drink.

Larry Randolph was also speaking. During his talk, John felt there were things he had to put right in his life. He went through those issues in his mind, committing them to God in prayer. Then he went to the back of the hall for a can of Coca-Cola. 'I strolled to the front where they were praying for people,' said John, 'and I was oblivious of the fact that I was "drunk". I was standing there, and I must have been swaying. One of the prayer team blew on me. Bang! I went on the floor.'

The drunkenness John was referring to was of the Holy Spirit, rather than of the alcoholic spirit variety. John was 'drunk' for much of his time in Toronto. 'I couldn't pack,' he said, 'my brother had to do that for me. I was drunk all the way through to the airport. We were the last on the plane. I staggered through customs. The funny thing was, two of us were drunk and one of us was sober. The one who was sober got pulled in at customs, while we staggered through. They kept him for 20 minutes!'

John found the symptoms would lift while at home, and he wasn't affected in meetings straightaway:

> I was hit by it at conferences, but not at church meetings until about six months into it. Then I suddenly began to get 'drunk' in church. I've been 'drunk' in meetings ever since. It's not just meetings. I can be 'drunk' while speaking to someone on the phone. I went to my nephew's wedding. I had a glass of orange juice in the foyer of the hotel and – bang! – on the floor I went. But the funny thing was, that side of the family would've never invited us to parties because we were evangelical Christians. Now they ask us along to all the do's because the Lord comes down and we have such a laugh and such fun!

Within the wider Church, however, John says that he has come to realize what it is like to be 'drunk' within a 'teetotal' society. 'What people forget is that John is not drunk as you suppose,' said Jean. She echoed similar comments from the book of Acts. When onlookers made fun of the early Christians and the signs of the Holy Spirit, Peter said, 'These men are not drunk, as you suppose. It's only nine o'clock in the morning!' Jean believes that this is the key issue. 'John feels it's like a cloak that comes down on him,' she said.

John explained:

You do things you wouldn't do normally. In New York, there was a woman on a stretcher. She'd had a ruptured disc for six months, was in a lot of pain, couldn't sit, and the only comfort she could get was to lie on this stretcher. But the way God touched her was through a prophetic drama. It was almost like the TV programme *ER*. And she ended up getting off the stretcher. There was another woman sitting on the front row who'd been really depressed. Her husband was concerned for her and took her everywhere to try to get her healed. All I can say is that the Spirit of God was there – it was nothing in us. The anointing was there. This woman just kept getting blasted out of her seat and laughing – almost as if she was in pain. She laughed for two or three days, and was healed. Her husband was crying. There was a lady with breast cancer who was healed in the meeting. Yet no one had laid hands on her.

It was obvious that a special course was being mapped out for his life, yet John found it difficult to be the focus of such attention. 'One thing that was painful was that God would always sort of "push" us to the front of a meeting – or near doorways. I thought,"Why do I do all this?" God said, "Do you see one of those flashing signs on the motorway, John? You're one of those. I don't hide you. I put you out where everyone can see you." I'm a sign.'

So how does he define his ministry? John's reply is simple, but effective. 'I go round the world serving drinks and having parties!' he said.

'Let me clarify that. I said to the Lord, "Lord, I don't want to say I'm a pastor because everyone's shutters come down because they're so miserable." That's the impression people get. The Lord said, "Well, just tell them you go round the world serving drinks and hosting parties!"'

So how about Jean in all of this? Has she been 'drunk' along with her husband? 'For John, it's been so radical, I was tending to look after him all the time,' she said. 'I'm able to look after him.' One particular night, Jean went back to their hotel room from a conference. 'God began to minister to me' is how she put it:

It was happening through the night. The Lord showed me various things – all completely different to what he'd done with John. He revealed different things to me. It was revelation. The Lord said we are different – we are chalk and cheese. But the Lord was doing that because many people couldn't cope with the way John was. Yet they could come up and ask me. That was the way God was doing it. We weren't meant to be the same. The Lord likes variety.

Many people don't actually realize that Jean is the wife of this 'drunk'. So she overhears passing remarks. 'I hear comments like, "Who does he think he is; there he is again, showing off; there he is, swanking again; he's always got to be seen."'

Jean explained how these people don't realize that such activity is actually *against* her husband's nature. 'It's completely contrary to his character,' she added. 'That's quite hard because especially among Christians you don't want to take glory and all that. Yet that's the one thing they tend to throw at you – you're trying to take the glory.'

The couple were reminded of a particular interpretation of the demise of the Welsh revival earlier this century. 'Jesse Penn Lewis was the one who accused Evan Roberts and said, "You're taking the glory from God." Straightaway that man backed away,' said Jean. 'Because of an accusation, the Welsh revival stopped. It's about letting God have his way – no matter what you're accused of – and just going for it.'

Jean has found that all Christian leaders want the conversion rate to go up in their churches and communities, but if
they were honest about it, many of them don't really want
the accompanying manifestations:

> They want it on their terms. People say the Church is
> going to be so different – it's going to be radical. Yet half
> the time they don't realize the way God is going to do it.
>
> It's not going to be in buildings. It's going to be out on
> the streets. It's going to be in places that are not 'acceptable'.
> And people aren't going to recognize it as church because
> it's not in a building. The next wave God will bring in will
> be so radical that many people aren't going to be able to
> enter into it. They won't be able to accept it. God wants
> to affect people out in the world, where they're at. Those
> people are crying out to God. He's hearing their prayers.
> And he will answer them. God wants to bring in the
> broken-hearted. He's hearing their heart cry. The Church
> as we know it now is not going to be recognizable.

Does Jean see any of that happening already? 'It's a trickle
at the moment,' she said. 'The second wave hasn't come in
yet, but God is preparing and breaking down walls. He's
given revelation to many.' So what is this 'second wave' Jean
talks about?

> I believe the second wave is when non-Christians will be
> drawn to things and God will be affecting them. I believe
> he's already preparing them now. I believe that many of
> the people in the first wave aren't going to be able to
> accept the second because it's going to be so radical. The
> 'unlovely' and 'rejected' will be looking for God.
>
> God is going to be raising those people up. And that
> includes those Christians that God has kept hidden.
> God has taken those people through so many trials and

different things because those people are going to be humble. And it won't be a false humility.

Jean believes that such people will become the 'fathers' of this movement. 'They are going to be so sensitive to these people who are coming in, the unlovely, they will know where they are coming from. I believe these people have been hidden for such a time as this.'

The Scotlands already have some experience of working with the rejected and outcasts of society. A former tent crusade evangelist, John went on to lead a church in Liverpool, which he described as 'a ministry to the poor'. Jean said, 'John was a pastor for 12 years at Bethesda which is between Anfield and Everton, in the city. It was an independent mission church. We always felt we wanted to do something with the poor and the downcast. We'd take clothes to refugee camps. Then we started up a charity shop and a soup kitchen. That's what was on our hearts.'

As John put it, 'We wanted to reach normal people. We didn't feel the Church related to the world. As one vicar explained, the Church's form of outreach was as if we were on one side of the chasm and people in the world were on the other. And now and again we'd chuck these tracts across to them. But we didn't really touch them.' As John and Jean reached out to the supposedly lower levels of society, their work attracted the attention of the upper levels, too. 'Although we were reaching the poor,' said John, 'the Lord opened up the doors to top people.'

Their community project won an award, and John was invited to St James's Palace to meet the Queen. He has also met Prince Charles and the Archbishop of Canterbury. 'It was just as if the Lord had opened doors,' said Jean.

But then despair hit them. 'Our workers came mainly from non-Christian sources,' said John, 'and turned out to be more dedicated than Christians. That's what was cutting us up, really.' At one stage they had up to 60 workers. 'Then what happened was that the Lord said to us he's going to do to us what he did to Gideon,' said Jean.

'We went right down in number to about 12 people. We were desperate, but the Lord said that was what he was going to do. Marc Dupont prophesied over us that God was going to release John from pastoral work and would open up doors for him. He'd be going to other countries.'

These days, John and Jean frequently travel to churches and conferences in Canada, North America and Scandinavia. They believe the phenomenon of being 'drunk' – although it has lasted for three years – will not affect John for ever. But there is deep irony in the very fact that it has happened at all and been a sustained experience for him: 'I became a Christian at 18. But an old lady had been praying for me since I was about nine, and she always said, "Never touch the drink." So my background is definitely teetotal,' he smiled.

7 *Lord of the dance*

It might be one of the most unconventional calls to worship, but it certainly has the desired effect. 'How ya'll feelin' out there?' cries rapper Cameron Dante. Rapper? Yes, Cameron is a former chart-topping artiste who turned his back on the godless elements of clubland and committed his life to God. Now he sings for the World Wide Message Tribe. 'Let me see your hands in the air,' he shouts.

Sure enough, the audience of young teenagers respond. And as the loud, pulsating beat suddenly slows down, a wave of worship sweeps across the ocean of hands that are raised high in adoration to God. Amid the ear-splitting sounds, frenetic video clips and energetic dancers, there is a tangible atmosphere of praise. Surprisingly, for a 30-something who doesn't frequent such events, I found it quite moving!

Looking around, it is obvious that the youngsters are caught up in something much bigger than themselves. Some may call it crowd control; others will write it off as emotional manipulation. But few can deny the fact that these dramatic dance displays of infectious 'in-yer-face' spiritual truth have been drawing in youth in their droves – and they are being turned on to Jesus – not sex, drugs and rock and roll.

The beat picks up again – so loud, you can feel it in your chest. The band demand that their audience answer one definitive question. 'Who's in the house?' they cry. 'God's in the house!' comes the youngsters' reply.

WWMT founder member Andy Hawthorne is perhaps the most unusual Anglican you'll ever meet. And he is probably one of the most fiery evangelists you'll ever hear, too. He gives a short message, literally spitting out the gospel with a strong Mancunian accent. His deep, gravelly voice makes you sit up and listen – this rapper is restless with the gospel. 'I wanted to be totally funky,' Andy says of the Tribe's approach. 'I wanted the means of communication to be up for grabs. But I wanted to be Bible-based. I wanted the message of the cross to be central to it.'

Andy's mother had become a Christian when he was three: 'So I went to church until I was about 11 – then sacked it as many kids do at that age. I completely rebelled as a teenager and got into all sorts of trouble until I was 17.' By that time his 'punk rock' brother Simon had forsaken his own rebellious ways after having a 'road to Damascus'-style conversion. He started talking to young Andy about God, and invited him to church. 'It wasn't a very exciting church, but what was exciting was the change in Simon's life,' said Andy. 'I spent a lot of time talking and reading books.'

At church, Andy heard his brother share the story of his own journey to faith. 'I then went home to my bedroom and asked Jesus into my life. Right from the word go, God gave me what I suppose is an evangelist's heart. I really, really got off on telling the gospel to people who didn't know Jesus. That's what made me excited.' Within a matter of months, Andy was being 'pushed forward' as the youth group evangelist.

'I spent years and years in a fashion accessories business with my brother, but spending as much of my spare time as I could preaching and telling people about Jesus in schools and churches.' There was a massive surge in the firm's turnover at this time. Business was booming; they needed extra staff urgently:

So we went to the Job Centre and said, 'Just send us some lads.' In a short space of time we took on 30-odd lads, or something ridiculous like that. But because we'd have anybody – we were so desperate – they gave us all the nutters no one else wanted to employ. What shocked us was not the fact that they smashed up a factory, fought with the foreman, graffitied everywhere and nicked all the stuff, but actually that they didn't know anything about Jesus. They really were pagans. They had no understanding of what it meant to be a Christian.

In the late 1980s Andy and Simon found themselves discussing the situation while attending a fashion fair. 'We were talking about these lads who were working for us, saying it can't be right – they just don't know anything about Jesus. It's not even that they've rejected the Christian faith – they just haven't had the opportunity.' Then they started dreaming dreams about reaching this post-Christian culture.

'We thought of booking the best rock theatre in Manchester, getting the best bands and putting on a kickin' presentation for these kids. Then we started saying we could get all the churches to work together under the same banner, get them to pray for one another – and all put on their own events in the build-up.'

That grand vision was born within just an hour's conversation. 'We felt the big finger of God come through the ceiling of this fashion fair,' said Andy.

I remember going home. I was reading through the Bible from cover to cover at that point. I was reading Isaiah 43 – which has become absolutely foundational to the work. It says there would be streams in the desert and rivers in the wasteland. Those things have become so much at the heart of what we're about. I had one of those experiences of God that I've had only a few times in my Christian life – where God really spoke 'big time' in that bedroom, saying, 'Mate, you're going to see this'.

Andy and Simon then made an appointment to meet Manchester's key church leaders. They really dressed up for the occasion. 'I remember us putting these big flashy suits on. We thought we'd impress them,' said Andy. 'But we were told we looked like a couple of spivs! We came in and told these guys, "you don't know us, but God's spoken to us, we want to encourage you to work together, we'll run it, we'll do the administration, we'll raise the money – if you just get your people behind it."'

Their efforts paid off. 'The Message' became the biggest youth mission Manchester had ever seen. More than 300 churches ran their own local evangelism in the build-up to a week at Manchester's Apollo Theatre. About 20,000 young people turned up. Hundreds made Christian commitments.

'It was one of those times where God really blesses something,' said Andy. 'Ministries sprang out of it. It was a cool time of God's blessing. At the end of it, me and Simon were knackered – and we also had a business that was knackered.' They decided they would take a year to put the business back on its feet, but something even bigger was waiting ahead of them.

With encouragement from a pop artiste friend Mark Pernells, a local charity, the Message To Schools Trust, emerged. 'We said at the start that we were going to make Manchester our priority,' Andy said, 'not because it's more special to God than anywhere else, but because there's so much need on the doorstep.' They would make schools a priority – 'because we'd seen that's where the kids were' – said Andy, himself a father of two children. 'We couldn't think of any other way to get to non-Christian teenagers.'

They took a small sound system around the schools in the

back of an estate car, and the work snowballed. From those humble beginnings, the Tribe have grown into a techno tour de force. They have become so popular on both sides of the Atlantic that they have had to live with the tension of stardom – plus their faithful commitment to youngsters in schools in Manchester. American interest grew when a single, 'The Real Thing', was selected by hundreds of top secular US radio stations. And despite having a direct gospel message, the song scooped number 22 position on Billboard's dance charts.

A recording deal with Warner Brothers followed. When the Tribe undertook an extensive five-week summer tour of the States, they played to nearly 250,000 Christian music fans. Yet the strong local commitment remained, and October 1997 saw the UK release of their album *Heatseeker* – targeted not only at the Christian scene, but also the secular market. An 18-track WWMT compilation *Revived* was released by Warner Alliance in the States – with the original version of 'The Real Thing'.

WWMT are hungry for a spiritual awakening in their home town, yet as far as they know, there's never been a revival there. But according to Andy, who is 36, they have certainly seen an accelerated response through assemblies, lessons and concerts:

> We're seeing something we haven't seen before – kids getting really fired up, moving on in God – but also more of them. Every time we went into a school in 1996, we were getting an average of 20 or 30 kids coming to faith. And obviously not all of them go on. But a significant number of them were going on, because we're working with decent churches. But in 1997 it's suddenly been like 50 to 100 – yet we're doing the same thing. Between two and four times as many people are responding as in the last four years.

Andy's conversation gets louder and more animated as he talks about his work, and his sentences are punctuated with expressions like, 'God's really fired us up'. The Tribe are driven by the prospect of a divine visitation in Manchester.

Their music booms with that passion. They are inspired by the 1949 Scottish Hebridean Islands revival – when 'it was hard to find a single person who wasn't seeking after God'. Someone sent them a copy of a tape, containing a message from Duncan Campbell – the evangelist at the heart of the Scottish awakening. The band's expert producer Zarc Porter sampled the preacher's monotone sermon, and worked it into a track. The result is a captivating, dramatic soundscape.

A key centre for the north-west of England, Manchester has been described as the dance music capital of Europe. It is also home for world-class football team Manchester United. But under the bright city lights lie areas of desperate social and spiritual need.

'Some of the stuff that goes on is unbelievable,' said Andy. 'We have the worst inner-city problems.' The Tribe have announced their plans for 'Eden' – a youth programme at Wythenshawe in the Greater Manchester area. Teams have been pioneering meetings and home groups in a very tough area on the largest council estate in Europe.

'In one sense it's scary,' said Andy. 'Three of our dancers moved into this horrible place. I was absolutely bottling it.' One couple linked to the project had several break-ins within the first few months of moving in. Andy says:

But one of the things God's really been saying to us is that we're going to be ministering in increasing tension – this tension between the triumphs and the pressure. The more you move into the triumphs, the more the pressure. I'm convinced the devil is absolutely brickin' it about what's going on in Wythenshawe. The kids we've seen so far are the worst cases from the most unbelievable families. And they're getting saved, filled with the Spirit and just going out there.

They feel it could be a prophetic example. 'If God can do it, not just with the hardest group of people – teenagers – but in the hardest place, Manchester, and in the hardest part of the city, anything's possible.'

One journalist from the United States spent the best part of a week watching the Tribe in action in Manchester's schools. He was researching a piece for one of America's top Christian youth magazines, *Breakaway*. And his verdict? 'I couldn't help thinking,' he later wrote, 'that I was standing on ground zero of a giant revival in northern England.'

If anyone was raised on revival, Southampton youth leader Billy Kennedy was. Billy recently led a big youth event at the city's football ground with the World Wide Message Tribe; his concerns and ambitions are very similar to theirs.

Billy's grandparents were converted at a tent meeting led by revivalist Edward Jefferies. They were convinced about the power of God when someone next to them, who was blind, suddenly had his eyesight restored.

'My grandparents started a meeting at their large house in Liverpool,' said Billy. 'I can remember it from my early days. Their home was always full of young people. There was a real move of God. Out of that group sprang a new church. That's been very much my roots and background.'

Billy's father was a leading footballer in Ireland. He enjoyed the attention of such clubs as Newcastle and Celtic – then he was dramatically converted and entered the ministry. He met Billy's mother at Bible College, and went on to lead a church that sprang out of the Jefferies revival. Billy was subsequently born in Liverpool in 1962. Later the family moved to Kilsyth near Glasgow – a community that has seen three major awakenings, the last being the 1904–6 revival.

'I can remember as a 14-year-old listening to a tape my dad had made,' said Billy. 'He was interviewing one of the last remaining survivors from that revival, and sharing about the prayer meetings with people prostrate on the floor. My dad has always had a thing about revival.'

In 1973 the Kennedys moved from Scotland to Northern Ireland – another region that has seen sporadic revivals down the ages. Billy attended secondary school in Banbridge, just south of Belfast. 'I think at some point I became a Christian,' he said. 'I can't really identify a time or a day when I gave my life to Jesus. But I tried to do it as often as I could, just to make sure!' His parents later moved back to Scotland while Billy stayed in Ulster to finish his A levels. 'But I got homesick – so I ended up moving back to Scotland to be with my parents.'

The education systems of Scotland and Northern Ireland were so different, though, that he didn't find it easy to switch schools. So he left school and got a job at a sports shop in Glasgow. Billy recalled that time: 'I can remember the day I started. God spoke to me and said, "I will bless you." I'd just turned 17. Within three months the manager had been sacked, and I was asked if I could run the shop for a couple of months. I ended up doing it for a year. And the takings increased dramatically. I was the 17-year-old manager of a shop with ten staff!'

Billy had developed a speech impediment in his teenage years, yet he realized that having to work in a shop and speak to people all day long was God's way of helping him overcome it. 'I'd never really been in any leadership position at school,' he admitted. 'I'd never been the captain of any team or anything like that. So I ended up having to learn to speak and lead in this shop environment.'

Business continued to boom, and the chairman of the company arranged to meet Billy. He can remember praying the night before his boss was due to arrive: 'God, if this guy says to me, "Mr Kennedy, what do you put your success down to?", I'll tell him it's all because of you.' The next day the two men were having coffee, and the chairman asked the very question that Billy had mentioned in his prayer. 'So I had to tell him it was God,' said Billy. 'Here was this 17-year-old lad telling the chairman of the company that he prays and God brings people into the shop and they buy things!'

While still working for the company, Billy left home and travelled around the country for a while. 'I ended up taking on a bit of a trouble-shooting role within the company,' he said, 'going for six months here, six months there, which was part of my training. I ended up going to Belfast, Cardiff, Liverpool and Bromley.' On his travels, he started to look at other churches. 'I'd been brought up in quite a non-charismatic set-up,' said Billy.

My parents are both very zealous for God and not very religious at all, but our church environments were non-charismatic. I began to go to various other churches. I went to a Pentecostal church in Belfast. Then I ended up staying with a Pentecostal couple in Cardiff and went to their church. I began to look at the whole thing of the baptism in the Holy Spirit. I was seeking.

Eventually Billy moved to the Southampton area in 1982, and worked at the sports shop in the city. He was just 19. He started attending the Community Church led by Tony Morton. At that point, they met as five smaller congregations:

The first week I was there, I went along to a house group meeting and found the whole thing quite difficult. People prayed for me, and began to prophesy over me – saying that I'd be a leader in the church, I'd be doing things that people in this room would be amazed by, that I'd be leading the people who are now leading me. And I'd never even had a prophecy before!

The next day Billy was sitting in his car. 'I got baptized in the Holy Spirit,' he said. 'I was speaking in tongues. Something exploded within me – and I was struck by the whole revelation of what salvation really meant, that my sins had been forgiven.' It was like someone had 'turned the lights on'. In those first three or four months after his experience, he 'devoured' Scripture and prayed 'non-stop'. 'It was just the most incredible thing.'

He was by now living in a flat above his workplace, and one day noticed all the young people milling about in the precinct below. 'I wept for people for the first time,' he recalled. 'I was reading about Paul being called to be an apostle, and I felt God saying, "That's what I've called you to be with these young people." But I didn't understand what an apostle was. That term had never been used in the churches I used to attend.'

Billy became heavily involved with the Community Church, and eventually left his retail job. He got married in 1984, and led an evangelistic team. Later he started working within the broader Cornerstone network associated with the church, and was then based back in Southampton. 'I was responsible for the youth work,' he said. 'We'd tried most things. We had Youth With A Mission, Youth for Christ and New Generation Ministries. I began to think we couldn't just have these big three-week missions. We had to have something more permanent.'

He toyed with the idea of a youth congregation. 'I thought that was something we needed to do,' he said, 'to give people identity and ownership.' In 1994 he went to South Africa and attended a youth congregation in Port Elizabeth. 'I saw it and thought, "This is what we want." It was 300 with-it young people, all really going for God in quite a dynamic way,' he said. Billy also met youth church pioneer Johnny Sertin, who was spearheading a similar initiative out of an Anglican church at Bournemouth. 'I thought, "We can do this, it's possible,"' he said.

That summer, in the wake of the 'Toronto Blessing', a team came over from Port Elizabeth and ran a youth camp for them. 'The kids just got blasted,' said Billy. 'Then all our youth leaders resigned. It was weird. It was through natural circumstances – people moving away, family commitments, work pressures, and so on. But we ended up with two of us trying to run our youth work. So it just collapsed.'

Word was spreading of a radical new youth worship event in West Sussex. 'Cutting Edge' was drawing hundreds of young people to a school hall in the quiet seaside town of Littlehampton. From just a small bunch of people experimenting with fresh approaches to worship, the event boomed. It became a top Sunday night spot for Christian young people from across south-east England.

It was different from anything else on the 'alternative worship' scene of the early 1990s. Other youth events around the country tended to be experimental 'Taizé-with-a-drum-machine' services. Cutting Edge was a time of extended 'indie'-style worship and a place where youngsters could just 'hang out' and talk about God. There would usually be a short, challenging sermon – but few other frills.

Initially, the key players were drummer and graphic designer Stewart Smith; recording studio manager Tim Jupp, who used to play keyboards for family worship pioneer Ishmael; and vocalist and recording engineer Martin Smith – who has written many popular worship songs. Later they became the chart band called 'Delirious?' – whose music has focused on young people's expectation for revival. Songs like 'Revival Town' hit just the right note for many fans.

Martin then met Billy Kennedy. 'They had this sense of

God wanting to do something in Southampton,' said Billy. 'We'd just closed down a big event here because of lack of interest. So we thought, "What's the point in doing another?" But I met Martin, Tim and Stuart. And it just seemed right that we should run with it.' So with two other churches initially, the Community Church launched a monthly youth worship event in the autumn of 1994.

A Wednesday night prayer meeting was started, to intercede for the youth work. 'So we had these two things running – this Wednesday evening prayer meeting, weekly, and this monthly Cutting Edge event that we didn't know what was going to be yet,' said Billy.

'Over the course of the next six months the Wednesday evening meeting just developed and grew into about 30 or 40 young people meeting together regularly to pray. The Cutting Edge event began to grow as well – attracting more people from outside and impacting them, giving them a new sense of freedom in worship.'

Billy realized that there was a lack of discipleship for the growing numbers. They looked at the question of breaking them down into smaller groups to make the job of pastoring them more manageable. 'So we did that, and split them into three small groups. We didn't quite know what we were going to do with them. Our friends in South Africa had begun to develop the cell model, so we got hold of the cell material and began to use it ourselves.' Three cell groups were launched at the end of 1995, with the young people pioneering the initiative themselves.

Cells are basically small groups, but with fundamental differences from the more conventional 'housegroup'-style meeting. 'Youth cells are peer led, mostly, whereas older housegroups were led by an adult,' said Billy. 'Cells are much more outward-looking and inclusive rather than being an exclusive group just for young people from the church. They are less programme-oriented and more people-oriented.

There's much more ownership.' Membership is kept between 8 and 12 people per cell. Once it gets much bigger, it splits to form two cells. Multiplication is the name of the game:

> Most of the cells last for six to eight months, so the cycle is quite short before it multiplies. The first couple of multiplications we did altogether. Now we've abandoned that idea and we just do it whenever it needs to happen. We're probably looking at at least one or two multiplications a month now. Cells have empowered the young people and created a structure for growth. It's helped them find an expression for their faith, so they've got things to do and not just be fed. It's created an environment for real discipleship rather than babysitting.

Cutting Edge also began to take off in 'a much more powerful way', said Billy. 'After the first year we were getting about 350. The second year we were getting about 600. We began to see some breakthroughs in salvation and healing.' A weekly celebration event called 'Sublime' had started for the young people. 'A band leads some worship, some of the young guys speak, then there's some form of response or ministry, then more worship and everyone goes home,' said Billy. 'So it's like a church meeting really – except the young people do it themselves. Each week two cell groups are responsible for planning and running it.' Sublime kept growing, too.

Billy is often asked how they integrate people from such a successful youth work, back into so-called 'main church'. He finds the integration issue an interesting one. 'People ask that question a lot,' he said. 'Often what they mean is, do they come on a Sunday? That's what they really mean – even though we say Church is not a building and Church is family. Yet in people's minds, if the kids don't come on Sunday morning, it hasn't worked. But I don't believe that's a criteria to judge success. However, about two-thirds of them come on Sundays.'

The young people play a part in leading the rest of the congregation in worship. Integration also happens at leadership level. 'When we have cell leaders' events, all of our youth cell leaders come as well. They are seen as leaders in the church and not just Sublime. A lot of the young people also play in the main worship band.'

Southampton's youth movement is changing the shape of Church, Billy believes. As the young people grow, the pattern of cell groups and celebration will be a way of life to them. 'I think it will radically affect the shape of Church,' he said, 'so the cell will take on much more of the focus of church – not Sunday meetings. Sunday meetings must serve the cells. So I think long term that is what's happening. It's to do with the future of Church – not just with youth work.'

Billy doesn't like to use the term 'youth worker' any more. 'If you ask me what I do, I'm not a youth worker – I'm a leader in the Church. That means I'm a leader of the next generation. We don't have youth workers – we have cell leaders and pastoral team leaders.'

He believes we should be looking at Church for the next generation. 'We have a whole people group worshipping, being discipled in a way that is appropriate and relevant to them,' said Billy, 'yet people mustn't be threatened by that.

'That is an element of the shape of the Church of the future. Sublime will begin to embrace more aspects of youth culture. I can see Sublime people developing their own record labels and fashion houses. So whether we end up with a huge organization called Sublime, I'm not sure. But out of that we will see a great variety of expression of the kingdom of God.' He has a vision of a vibrant, living community – rather than just a group of people meeting in a church building.

'God has done something within this generation. We'll see the benefit come through in a decade or two with regards to what Church is, and its mission focus,' he said. 'There's an incredible bubbling and simmering of the life of God among this generation. The more you travel, the more you see it. It's a phenomenal thing. It will transform our nation. Even if we maintain the momentum we've had the last three years, we'll do it. Even if there isn't another major outpouring of any sort, what will happen in three or five years' time will be significant.'

Southampton's young people aren't superhuman, however. Billy admits they have their own hang-ups:

> But within the core there's a zeal for God and a desire for holiness that's just incredible.
>
> We've talked about the whole area of relationships. At the beginning they were all pairing off. So we said, 'What are we going to do about this? If we're looking to welcome people who aren't Christians and who've been hurt, rejected and abused, how do we create an environment where they can come in and feel safe, and not be pounced upon?' So together we came up with this idea that going out is about getting married. So don't bother. The result is that out of nearly 200 teenagers in Sublime, there's only a handful of couples.

Billy thinks that outcome is 'amazing'. Outsiders are often shocked by the arrangement – although no law has been laid down. Billy explained:

> We've got some fringe people who like courting. This girl arrived, made some form of commitment and one of our fringe guys by the end of the meeting was snogging her outside. I was furious. It was just unacceptable. So it really prompted us to say, 'What are we going to do? We're going to get needy young people coming in, expecting safety – and they'll just get abused again.'

Therefore they have created an environment where virtually the norm is singleness and close friendships – but hardly any kissing and cuddling. The pressure to pair off has been broken.

'It's not a rule,' said Billy, 'it's just that we made these helpful suggestions. But it does seem to have an impact. Going out is not a recipe for marriage. It's a recipe for divorce. You get married, you fall out, you divorce – because that's what you've always done. You've spent ten years doing that when you were going out. But now their hunger for God and for holiness is just phenomenal.'

Billy believes God's timing is in it all:

When the whole Toronto thing happened there was the generation who'd been in the charismatic renewal, and they were refreshed. But there was a whole generation that weren't around before and who got ignited for the first time. That's what has been happening.

Thirty years ago it was mostly young people in the charismatic renewal. Many had to leave their churches mainly to form the new churches. The traditional Church couldn't cope with what was happening. So they didn't have a body in which to be formed and cared for. Thirty years ago the body wasn't in place. Now the body is there. So we can operate fully within this church and almost be church within church. But it's like we are an embryo within the womb. We've got that safety, that protection, that covering, and we can grow and develop and learn. That's why it's not just youth work. It's Church for this generation. For the first time it's in place.

It is an unprecedented time in this nation's spiritual history, Billy feels – 'which is why this generation is so crucial. The young generation needs to take hold of responsibility,' said

Billy, 'and those who are older need to train them. It's quite a brave man that can say, "This is the revival generation." We're talking about a whole generation turning the nation around. It's not going to happen overnight.'

8 *Celtic awakenings*

There were hushed tones; and under the loud colours of the big top, careful hands silently selected pieces of red, white or blue wool. As the prayerful returned to sit on the grassy floor, they reflected on their response to the vivid imagery.

Red referred to the pain of 'blood martyrdom'. White meant abandoning earthly desires for the sake of loving God. Blue was for those who longed to retreat and give themselves to prayer and fasting. Some knelt down in the dirt, deep in devotion. Others whispered words of encouragement to one another. Whatever their reaction, they were all considering the call to become 'living martyrs', laying down their lives continually for God. Those were the closing scenes to the controversial 'New Celts' presentation at the popular annual Greenbelt Christian arts festival.

Celtic spirituality has been a fringe feature of British church life for some time, but there has been an explosion of interest in recent years. Deep, intertwining strands of the Celtic mindset that once lay dormant are rising up and being woven again into the fabric of the twenty-first-century Church. And that's true right across the Christian spectrum – from quiet liberal to wild charismatic.

Peace and justice, human rights, love of creation, art and culture – all those issues were important to the Celts, and they're being revived today. Something that deeply impacted the life and culture of these islands long ago is re-emerging and finding new favour in the postmodern world – a world that has effectively dethroned the idea that 'modern' is best.

What makes this latest expression different is the way it is presented in a popular context and style. Through the New Celts, stories from the Age of the Saints are told amid a powerful setting of music, dance and drama. A compelling mix of traditional and contemporary sounds conveys both the reflective and risky elements of the lifestyles and ministries of the early Celtic missionaries.

'Celtic music seems to be striking a fresh chord with many people at the moment,' the programme notes say, 'not just in its traditional forms but also within dance culture.' Frenetic fiddle playing, moving poetry and intense narration produce a dramatic display. The haunting sound of Uileann pipes floats across a thumping electronic backbeat. 'There's a sacrifice in following Jesus,' Maggie Ellis tells the Greenbelt crowd. 'Are you prepared to push through the pain barriers?'

Maggie and her husband Roger are members of the leadership team at Revelation Church, Chichester, where the New Celts initiative was first drafted and developed. They were formerly the youth group of a local Anglican church who discovered the power of God in a new way. They left to form their own charismatic church, which has since become established as a major renewal centre on the south coast of England. More recently, they have been deeply enriched and inspired by tapping into this ancient stream of Celtic Christianity.

'The New Celts is a message literally for the Celtic tribes,' says Roger, 'but it also goes further and acts as a stimulant for churches to move out and establish the life of Jesus in the ethnic and indigenous groups that surround us.' He refers to the 'aboriginal apostles' of these islands – which included people like Brendan, Columba, David and Cuthbert. 'God wants us to uncover these roots,' he adds, at a point in the presentation where the beat gets faster. 'There is an indigenous British Church. Its spirituality awaits our discovery.'

Roger describes his personal journey into Celtic ways as 'one of the most dynamic encounters with God I've ever had'. He took time out three years ago to reflect on it all. The result was a transformation for him and his church. Roger noticed how this ancient movement captured a biblical and Jesus-centred spirituality. 'That's how the issue of the Celts first hit me,' he said at Greenbelt. 'They were incredibly successful in the way they captured the imagination of the people at grassroots.' The ancient Celts had to face a pagan culture; and so Christians today can learn from them, he explains, as they tackle a postmodern pagan culture.

Deep within his own country's history, Roger discovered the radical saints who pioneered a holistic spirituality. The Celts left an example of mission and lifestyle that churches can translate and 'remix' into the twenty-first century. 'We have to take the truth that we have, and keep the fundamental rhythm,' he said. 'But we remix it for this generation.' The Celts did just that – they planted communities, encouraged deep friendships, honoured women, were at ease with creation, and 'lived in a dynamic experience of God's power'.

Renewed by their discovery, Roger, fellow leader Chris Seaton, and their church's worship team developed the 'New Celts' presentation. It was first shown at a Pioneer leadership conference in 1996. Wherever it is performed, audiences are challenged to make a deeper commitment to God, as Roger and Maggie urge them to follow the Celtic call to a life of sacrifice.

A number of the early saints were of noble birth or even royal ancestry, but they gave it all up for a greater treasure. 'They had an incredible sense of adventure,' Roger said. 'However, the costs were high. They set off in rudderless coracles – at the mercy of tides and currents. The Holy Spirit was the wild wind who blows where he wishes. He cannot be domesticated.'

The presentation has attracted some criticism – particularly from those concerned about so-called 'New Age' influences. But it has also re-awoken something deep within the hearts of others who have been watching and listening. People are recognizing that here was a pre-Reformation Church endowed with power from on high.

Careful not to destroy what God can use, the ancient Celtic Christians would embrace culture as well as confronting it. They would purify pagan sites. To them, life was a never-ending, intertwining pattern, as the Celtic knot demonstrates. Elements of art and culture could be 'recycled' – not rejected. That is a powerful, relevant message to a twenty-first-century world.

The Celtic Church wove itself into the cycle of art, culture and community. The gospel infiltrated and was imbibed by the common life. British, Irish and American believers alike are now revisiting the faith of the ancient Celts – and finding a new dynamism for the future. There have been reports of this spiritual movement attracting interest from even further afield, from the USA and even Switzerland – another country with its own links to the Celts – and allegedly from Australia and Africa.

It is significant that 1997 – said to have been the 'year of the Lord's favour' by those with an interest in the prophetic – was also the 1400th anniversary of the death of Columba. Prophet, poet, priest and prince – Columba was all of those. He had a major impact on religion, art and literature that continues to this day. Among the best known of Celtic saints, in AD 563 he set up a pioneering mission base on the tiny island of Iona.

'Iona' is an evocative word. The name conjures up images of a windswept, mystical and romantic isle off the west coast of Scotland. It speaks of ancient stone crosses overlooking a sandy coastline. Formed from some of the oldest rocks in the world, it was a major bridgehead for one of the first gospel invasions of these islands. From there, Columba and his disciples spearheaded a massive spiritual and cultural revolution that spread across much of the known world.

Sent into exile from Ireland, Columba spent the last 34 years of his life based on Iona – which even today can only be approached by passenger ferry from the larger island of Mull. If the weather is bad, and the boat cannot sail, the unsuspecting visitor can be marooned there for a few days! Yet from that small community, an immense outflow of spirituality and academic learning has poured down through the ages. It is thought that the *Book of Kells*, reckoned to be one of the most precious treasures of the Western world, was written there.

Monks from Iona set up mission outposts in other regions. Columba and his intrepid evangelists have been credited with spreading the Christian faith to Scotland, the north of England and into Europe. Playwright and Celtic enthusiast Murray Watts has been working on a screenplay of the life of Columba, and recently compiled a book of the saint's own writings. 'Columba's character is associated with miraculous powers, prophetic wisdom, the crowning of kings and the spread of Christianity throughout Ireland and Scotland,' said Murray. 'He can justly be called one of the founding fathers of the Scottish nation and, in many ways, its true patron saint.'

Described as a courageous man, almost warlike at times, Columba preached to people who were under the influence of Druid opponents of Christianity. But his faithfulness was rewarded as kings and rulers became converted, and the gospel spread throughout Scotland and northern England. Columba died in the year 597, but ever since pilgrims have been descending on Iona to remember him and to give thanks for his remarkable ministry.

It was said of Columba: 'He had the face of an angel; he was of an excellent nature, polished in speech, holy in deed, great in counsel . . . loving unto all.' Columba is now being seen as part of the 'so great a cloud of witnesses' that started with the heroes of faith of Bible times. Some Christians have been praying specifically for a holy restlessness – the kind that the Celtic Christians had – and for a sense of their own inadequacy, leading into a complete and utter dependence on an unseen God, who they believe will triumph over the wicked forces that have invaded their land.

Mary Robinson's past presidency of Ireland has been seen as a time of boosting that country as a secular state within Europe. Yet when she undertook an official tour of Scotland, she announced that she was tracing the different stages of the life of Columba. 'I want my journey to Scotland to be a pilgrimage,' she told the media at the outset, 'and I want the trip to have a strong ecumenical dimension.'

Thus Celtic Christianity is being born again in the hearts of believers, and that includes 'traditional' and charismatic Christians – throughout both Great Britain and Ireland. They are inspired by this indigenous spiritual movement that deeply impacted these islands, and then spread across a whole continent. Celtic monks travelled through the remains of the old empire and beyond, living and sharing the life of the gospel. They included many other strategic people with apostolic ministries. From the community on Iona, less than 40 years after Columba's death, an Irish monk named Aidan was sent to the kingdom of Northumbria to bring the gospel of the people of King Oswald. He set up base on another tiny island, Lindisfarne.

The mysterious mantle had obviously been extended to his ministry – as Aidan and this little chunk of rock called Lindisfarne were to have a massive influence on the English race. He became known as the 'apostle of England', and today is credited with being first among England's evangelists. With the rising interest in Celtic saints, some people have sought to follow in Aidan's footsteps. Others have been 'called' to do it.

Lindisfarne hardly seems a centre of action. It is cut off from the mainland by tides twice a day, on a rock just big enough to accommodate a modest community of 130 people and a school with only one pupil. Yet 57-year-old Ray Simpson and his island home are very much in demand. Half a million people each year descend on Lindisfarne, and some of them look to Ray to help them tap into the ancient stream of spirituality that flows through this region. For here is England's 'cradle of Christianity', where the faith of the nation's forefathers found fresh expression and meaning from a remote mission base that impacted much of the country.

Ray is a gentle, warm and friendly man. A small wooden cross hangs from his neck, resting in the folds of a chunky jumper. An ordained Anglican minister, Ray runs Christian retreats on Lindisfarne, writes books and other resources on Celtic spirituality, and may even consider becoming a temporary 'soul friend' if you ask him nicely. This is a man who takes people's needs seriously – and who wants to guide them down the ancient paths of England's deep spiritual heritage. In fact, many of the present-day pilgrims who flock to his island base often say they have the feeling of 'coming home', as they drink from the well of Christianity in that place.

'When I came here a year and a half ago, interest in this Lindisfarne Retreats ministry was like a cloud the size of a person's hand,' he told me. 'But people are now coming from all over the world. We've had people from America saying, "This is where we belong."' Ray believes that among the key features of the early Church on these islands were its emphasis on community, hospitality, a sense of journey – and a signs and wonders ministry. 'That's relevant for well into the next century,' he said. One Cambridge professor told him the headings of Ray's book, *Exploring Celtic Spirituality*, provided the agenda for the next generation! Quite a commendation. 'I was very humbled,' said Ray, 'and amazed!'

Many roads lead to Lindisfarne. All kinds of people end up there from all kinds of places – with all kinds of stories to share. One man suffering from cancer was given a year to live, and spent some of his last precious days on Holy Island. 'Often they're very loyal Christians,' said Ray, 'but feel their church is missing out on whole dimensions. They want to think it through. They're trying to find rhythm. They want their personal and church life to be based on rhythm rather than pressure. They want to give up half the things their pastor wants them to do.'

A man travelled up from London after the Samaritans had recommended that he visit Lindisfarne. He wasn't a Christian, but spent much of his stay there building a 'cairn' – a memorial of rough stones – to represent the issues that were troubling him.

Four people came from a Vineyard church in Oslo, Norway. Ray explained that their violent ancestors, the Vikings, had come to Lindisfarne centuries before – and took some of the young monks back to Norway. There they became evangelists. Now these twentieth-century Norwegians wanted to spend eight days on retreat on Lindisfarne, and understand more about Celtic spirituality.

'That was a wonderful time,' said Ray, 'they ministered to me, too!' One of them prayed that Ray would make plenty of money through his books. The next day, requests for three bulk orders arrived! That kind of news is always welcome at Ray's house, for he 'lives by faith'. In practice that means he is living on less than half of what he earned as a fully paid minister on the mainland – 'so it's a bit hairy,' he said.

There is no doubt that Lindisfarne is meeting some deep spiritual needs. Ray himself was first drawn to the place in 1988; he was on sabbatical when someone mentioned to him that he should go there – 'which I'd never thought about in my life before'.

Before coming to Lindisfarne, Ray had been in charge of a project in Bowthorpe, Norwich, establishing an 'oasis of love' for people who were hurting. That had been his mission for

18 years. Ray felt drawn towards living on Lindisfarne, but he had normally visited in the summer when it looks at its best. So he had to ask himself the question, was this feeling more than just romanticism? 'I knelt down on the cold earth and offered up this land and myself to God,' he recalled. It was a turning point.

'I knew nothing could ever be the same again. God was saying, "I want a cradling approach where my people are close to the land, close to the people and close to the supernatural."' Unconditional hospitality and simple lifestyle would be key themes. Ray shared his experience with Anglican renewal leader Michael Mitton. 'He and others were interested and felt God was speaking along similar lines. We all linked up, and for two years we met quarterly to develop a way of life based on Celtic spirituality. That led to us launching in March 1994 what we now call the Community of Aidan and Hilda.'

The name of the community reflected their desire to put men and women in balance. Other community members anointed Ray with oil and prayed over him to be released. 'Someone spoke in a tongue. The interpretation was a picture of a coracle all ready and waiting. I just had to step into it.'

After two years, with his bishop's blessing, Ray resigned as vicar and team leader at the church in Bowthorpe, which had been his family for so many years, and went to live on Lindisfarne. A small house became his base – accommodating a private chapel, library and guest room. A registered charity called the Lindisfarne Mustard Seed Project was then formed to support Ray's ministry. It would also further his long-term aim of setting up a community on the island itself, building on the foundations laid by Aidan many centuries before. Ray had embarked on an important new phase of his own spiritual journey:

Someone said to me it's very important that you go to the

island just to be – and to learn to be still. She also said, 'I had a picture of you on Cuthbert's Island [a little rock you wade out to] with a full moon shining on you, and there is a total stillness. In that total stillness of your being, you are deeply transformed, and out of that will come your ministry.' She also said, 'You're not to come with your own blueprint to the island.'

Ray was welcomed to Lindisfarne by David Adam, the island's resident vicar, poet and pilgrim leader. 'He helped me to understand the presence, being aware of God's presence. Every day in God's creation is unique and different. Every sun rising and sun setting is something uniquely special from God for me.'

The island's changing seasons seemed to say something of Ray's spiritual state. 'I wanted to jump from November to spring,' he said, 'but God said to me, "Journey into the dark of November, get to know your shadow – and embrace it." That was important to me. I practised being on my deathbed, being ready to die. So I became deeply fulfilled with being in this place – even in the depths of winter.' Ray is very much aware of his environment and his fellow islanders. 'I knew it was important to treat every islander as my family, and to be sensitive and supportive of the different Christians and groups on the island,' said Ray, 'to honour them and not to tread on their space.'

So what of the future? 'God knows,' said Ray, quite literally meaning it.

But I'll tell you of my heart's desire. Whether it's God's will remains to be seen: that Lindisfarne will be a community whose significance is as great as the original little community of Aidan in the seventh century, providing a mission to the people of the land, hospitality, learning, creative arts, and an experience of spirituality for people who have written off the Church. I want to offer an experience of a rhythm of prayer and work in which the ordinary, daily life of the island is a valued part – not divorced from it. We need more facilities that are island-friendly and humble.

On his deathbed 1,400 years ago, Columba prayed for unity. 'See that you be at peace among yourselves, my children, and love one another,' he said. 'Follow the example of good men of old, and God will comfort you and help you, both in this world and in the world which is to come.'

That plea from the year 597 echoes right down the ages to today. It has found its way into popular culture – particularly through the music of bands like Iona and Caedmon's Call. At the forefront of the Celtic awakening that has touched churches across Great Britain, the band Iona mix electronic and traditional instruments to produce a dramatic landscape of sound. They have already positioned themselves as one of Europe's bestselling Christian bands. Their last studio album, *Journey into the Morn*, was even applauded by the secular music press. *Q* magazine featured them as one of their 'Best 50 Albums of the Year' in January 1997, and they have been named among the top five folk bands in the world.

Among their best loved compositions is the stunning 'Irish Day' – a tribute to Columba. The lyrics of that song bring hope to Britain, made up as it is of the great Celtic nations: 'It is here that time has granted/That the light should still burn on/It was here a seed was planted/In the brave heart of an Irish son'. Their musicianship shines. Their music touches an ancient vein, crossing cultures and encouraging people to sing and dance in unity.

The American group Caedmon's Call took their name from a Northumbrian saint who worked as a farm servant, then as a lay brother to the community of Whitby. God may have given him the gift of song, for history records that he was the first of the Anglo-Saxons to write in verse. He had no natural talent for singing – and reportedly ran away from occasions when it was required. Yet all that changed when he heard the voice of God telling him to sing. He refused, but the voice persisted. And when he opened his mouth, Caedmon sang verses that had never been heard before. Many singers and songwriters followed him, but none could match the songs he wrote. 'It's a real story,' said founder member of Caedmon's Call, Cliff Young:

> Caedmon lived in the seventh or eighth century. The odd thing was, we had all heard that story for the first time within a week. It's amazing that we all heard this rather obscure story in that same period of time. We have gone through times when we wanted to change the name. But in playing college venues we realized it was the right kind of name. It's part of the whole draw and interest of the band.

Caedmon's Call play their own brand of contemporary folk music, though not necessarily 'Celtic' in sound. They grapple with practical discipleship issues.

Celtic Christianity has become 'flavour of the year' – as Anglican renewal pioneer Michael Milton put it. 'We must give it time to see whether it's just a craze,' he said, 'or if it's something deeper that can profoundly affect the life of the Church.' Mitton has seen much enthusiasm for Celtic spirituality across the Anglican Church. 'And I get letters from all denominations,' he said. 'There's quite a diversity showing an interest.'

Many people have been discovering *pre-Christian* Celtic spirituality – particularly with the New Age explosion focused on places like Glastonbury. What they might not fully appreciate is that it was followed by this dynamic gospel movement that swept across these islands – and other nations – with its life-changing message. The great saints of old – who pioneered New Testament Christianity in ancient Britain – have left their footprints for us to follow. They have left their wells for us to re-open and drink from.

The spirit of adventure, of abandonment, of all-or-nothing commitment – which gripped the ancient Celtic Christians and caused them to confront the pagan status quo of their time – is a legacy that inspires us today. It's the call of the wild. It echoes through the caverns of history to the cold light of today. You can see it in the popularity of such secular rock bands as Clannad and Runrig – and the hit musical shows *Riverdance* and *Lord of the Dance*.

Places like Iona and Taizé draw hundreds of people every year searching for a quiet time of retreat and reflection. There is both a calling back and a calling forwards. For not only are people retracing the steps of ancient saints back through the ages, but also they're responding to the radical call of the Celts who believed wholeheartedly in mission.

That sense of adventure took the Irish monk Aidan to Scotland where he was trained, and on to England in 635 – where he sparked the evangelization of a nation. Aidan cared for the poor and bought slaves in order to give them freedom. He was the 'people's saint', as Ray Simpson believes.

When Princess Diana died, several people said, 'Do you think there is significance that she died on St Aidan's Day?' He was the people's saint, and she was the people's princess – and Aidan is an anagram of Diana. The more I thought about it, the more I thought that the response to Diana's death shows the people of the land are, in a way, longing to worship. They're longing to come, but they just need to be facilitated.

Ray pointed out how the Church of England had risen to that challenge in its way, by hosting Diana's funeral service. 'I feel God is saying to us, through Aidan, "facilitate this".' Like a resounding echo from the past, Celtic Christianity offers to fill the spiritual void of these islands.

Most people collapsed, their arms stretched out as if grabbing the hilt of a sword. It was an astonishing sight. 'I believe this is the message of the sword of God's deliverance over Scotland,' said John Arnott, pioneer of the so-called 'Toronto Blessing'. 'You've had years of fighting among yourselves and others. Now it's time to fight the enemy of your souls.'

People had lined up for 'ministry time, Toronto-style' – often regarded as the most interesting part of a renewal/revival meeting! John and his wife Carol walked along each line, praying for people, and handing out the invisible 'blades'. Carol told the packed hall in Stirling how she believed she had been given a prophecy about equipping people with a 'golden sword'. The cry was to throw away the means of the past. God had a better way.

'The old methods are not acceptable to me any more,' said Carol as she read out her prophecy in the first person, 'because I am doing a new thing. This new way is not the old. My sword is made of pure gold. If you wield it, the captives will be set free, the chains will be broken.'

Delegates at the 'Scotland Ablaze!' conference were being urged to purify their lives. Carol continued in the first person: 'In this next wave, I am requiring those who take up this golden sword to be refined, to be pure, and to have all the dross refined in the fire. Because if you take this sword and there's secret sin in your life, it will kill you.'

Shaking violently – a 'manifestation' or 'response' of the renewal – she added, 'This next wave is no joke. It's not a laughing matter.' God is a warrior, she pointed out, referring to a passage in the book of Exodus, 'I have called you as a warrior nation.' People had turned their gifting against each other, said Carol. The words carried much meaning for the nations that make up the United Kingdom – where prejudice, division and intertribal warfare have been rife for centuries.

'But the Lord God is your father, and you are his sons and his daughters. You are mighty warriors because that's what God has put in you – mighty men and women of valour. You can do the exploits that God has called you to do.' People were crying out from across the big meeting hall. 'You will be the bravehearts of the Lord.'

The importance of a pure life was underlined. 'The warning in this prophecy,' said Carol, 'is the secret sin that God has been trying to talk to you about for months, for years. God is calling a bride that's pure and holy, a bride that's passionately in love with Jesus – but not a bride that's perfect – because you will make mistakes.' It is the secret, hidden things people should be concerned about right now, she explained, like pornography, jealousy, gossip and lying.

The Arnotts are ordinary people at the forefront of an extraordinary movement. Growing up within the Baptist denomination, John attended Ontario Bible College; and long before the 'Blessing' broke out, he was a businessman. He ran a couple of shops, farms and a travel business. 'I sure learned about growing a few things,' he smiles, reflecting on those days. But his real desire was to work within the Church.

He married Carol, and together they went on an outreach to Indonesia. After returning to Canada, they set up a church in Ontario as part of John Wimber's Vineyard movement – an international network of charismatic churches. Then came the work at Toronto, where they became involved on a full-time basis. When the renewal hit, it caused a split in the Vineyard movement at the time, and the Toronto church pulled out of the network.

What may surprise some is the fact that both John and Carol are divorcees. The positive side is that they both feel they can relate to many of the people they care for – who themselves have come through broken marriages. Their mission statement has become famous: 'Walk in God's love, then give it away.'

They brought that message to Stirling. For some Scots, the town is just another stop on their train journey home. Yet the place has symbolic importance. From medieval times it was, strategically, the most significant place in Scotland. Whoever held Stirling, controlled the nation.

Its dramatic cliff-top castle – built on a volcanic rock overlooking the town – was ideally placed to command this narrow gap in the country's heartlands, through which ran all the major north–south routes. From its battlements, the town's defenders would have had a panoramic view of the surrounding terrain. So the town became known as the 'brooch' or 'clasp' of Scotland. It was the key to the kingdom.

It was against this historic backdrop that 'Scotland Ablaze!' was held at the town's Albert Halls in the summer of 1997. Even as delegates started arriving on a warm Saturday afternoon, people were displaying the so-called 'manifestations' that have become a hallmark of the renewal movement of the 1990s.

During the introductory worship time, which opened with the song 'Send Your Power O Lord', some were becoming visibly unsteady on their feet – almost as if they were intoxicated. Charismatics use the phrase 'drunk in the Spirit' to describe such phenomena, interpreting it as being full of the 'new wine' of God, swooning under the influence of his love and power. The Blaze Band, from Surrey, led the worship with a song called 'His Banner Over Me Is Love'. Towards the back, a couple of delegates fell back into their chairs, laughing.

'It's good to have fun in the presence of the Lord, isn't it,' conference organizer Tony Black declared from the stage. 'I had 32 years of religion – and now we have freedom!' There was much applause. Tony, who is 42, asked where people had travelled from. Delegates indicated that they had come from places as diverse as England, Ireland, Brazil, Wales, New Zealand, Canada, the United States, Norway and the Shetland Islands. 'The Lord's got a banquet prepared for us today,' Tony told them all.

Then he explained that the main speakers, John and Carol Arnott from Toronto Airport Christian Fellowship, were on their way; that there was a 30-strong dance troupe from Brazil called Viva Vive; and a 'ministry team' of over 70 ready to pray for people at the end of the main sessions.

But most of all, Tony added, 'the king of glory is coming to Scotland. He's already here – but he's coming in great power. There's so much that God wants to do, and he is riding in. He's shown so many that we've been talking to, a mighty army that he's raising up, and that mighty army consists of a bunch of nobodies from nowhere.' Tony clearly feels that 'ordinary' people will be used in significant ways in revival.

Tony has Scottish roots; he was an army child, born into a Scottish regiment based at the time in Germany. But he speaks with a very 'proper' English accent. That's probably down to the fact that he was later educated at a public school in southern England. He travelled around a lot with his family – living in Africa, Europe and the United States at different periods throughout his formative years.

When just seven, Tony had a supernatural vision. 'Christ came into my room,' he recalled, 'and he was feeding the five thousand. The parable of the five thousand is quite simply that Jesus would do something out of nothing. He would provide in seemingly impossible situations.' Tony had always wondered if there was a deeper message to his experience, but has come to realize 'there's no meaning other than that

God's love and provision for his children is of paramount importance'.

Tony had loving parents, though it was a 'turmoiled upbringing'. He was abused at school. As he grew older, he chose to pursue a lifestyle of drink and drugs. Aged 24 and at his 'lowest ebb', he had another 'encounter with God' – while driving his Ferrari! Later he married Annette, and took over the running of a multi-million pound leisure centre. However, they were encountering staff problems: 'I discovered that the cleaners weren't only cleaning,' he remembered. 'They were alleged to be stealing as well. Several of them were from a coven of witches nearby. So when I didn't renew their contract, they cursed me and my wife. And within six weeks, all sorts of evil things had happened.' Tony and Annette split up, and his parents wouldn't even talk to him. He looked for help in churches, but for a couple of months he didn't find the answers he needed. Some ministers told him simply to go away, and that there was 'no such thing as witchcraft'.

Tony and Annette were later reunited. 'One day I found this lovely gentleman in his eighties, who said, "Yes, you've been cursed." He took me in and mentored me. He took me into his church, cleaned me up, and sent me off to Oxford to train for the ministry.' The curse was broken, and things improved. 'The power of the devil was broken through prayer,' he said.

It was 1980 when the couple moved to Oxford, and found a charismatic Baptist church – where he 'got absolutely blitzed by the Holy Spirit'. That was Tony's first experience of the gifts of the Spirit, as practised in charismatic fellowships across the country. But he didn't follow through the idea of formal ministry training. 'I felt God was calling me to stay in business,' he said, 'so I did.'

It was while attending an independent fellowship that Tony received a 'prophetic word' which said, 'God has actually put you on the right track, and sent you to the university of the Holy Spirit.' It was a 'precious time,' he recalled. 'It was in a village in the middle of nowhere just outside Oxford. And they were lovely people.' Four years later they were on the move again and lived in Warrington for a while.

In 1986 Annette experienced 'strange manifestations'. Tony didn't like it: 'I thought it was odd, and I'm afraid my heart was a little hardened to it – which is true for many people. They find it difficult to deal with. But at the end of the day it was God challenging my mind to expose my heart. Even then I'd become fairly set in a routine.'

With a group from Argentina, Tony was helping to plant a church in Southsea. He was also invited to become the founding director of an organization called CareLine that looked after carers of the terminally ill in Southampton.

He helped to set up CareLine's operation, but in 1989 he was offered a job with the Leprosy Mission, one of Britain's leading Christian-based charities. 'Two years later I was promoted to become one of the executive directors,' he said. He also became a member of the international general council. That meant being more involved in overseas work. 'One of my greatest joys was visiting more than a dozen countries – on occasion with Princess Diana, who was our patron then. I'd also grown up in the same village as her family and got to know them a little. She was a seeker, and had a lovely heart.'

Tony's work with the Leprosy Mission gave him a heart for the poor. 'If you have leprosy, there's no worse way to suffer,' he explained. 'It's the worst disease in the world. You suffer – body, soul and spirit. All five senses get absolutely shattered. Then you get rejected. Then you get told you've been cursed by the gods and you're on the way to hell. If you get leprosy, you're a total write-off.' Meeting those who suffer in such horrific ways has caused Tony to mix his charismatic faith with social concern.

'But it's more than social action. It's much more. I call it "full reconciliation" – body, soul and spirit. We want to see these people physically healed, we want to see them emotionally healed, we want to see them spiritually healed, and we want to see them socially rehabilitated.' Then with retraining, such people can be restored to their communities – instead of living a shadowy existence as outcasts from society.

Tony yearns for the miraculous, and that's partly because he has experienced it. In 1991 he was visiting a hospital in Nepal. The location was in the middle of nowhere, 20 miles outside Katmandu, and a gift from the king. The hillside had been a refuge for people with leprosy, and considered by the locals to be cursed. 'They were happy to give it to us,' said Tony. 'It was my first overseas visit.'

One evening he accompanied the surgeons on a ward round. They were going from bed to bed, checking the patients. Among them was a young man with a disfigured stomach – and crippled with leprosy, cancer and tuberculosis. Tony asked a female doctor what the prognosis was. She just lifted her hands in resignation.

'She moved on to the next bed,' he recalled. 'Then for the first time in my life, a sense of indignation came over me. I felt this overwhelming gut-wrenching feeling.' The sensation was so strong that it made him double up as if in pain. 'I put my hand on to the man's head, and I felt this power come through the top of my head, into my chest, through my heart and down my left arm – into this boy's head. He jumped in the bed.' The doctors had moved on, so no one witnessed Tony's unusual bedside manner.

Two days later, Tony was preaching in the chapel. 'In the third row on my right-hand side was this young boy – with the biggest grin on his face – and no lump on his stomach. He was healed.'

It was in 1993 that Tony returned to the land of his fore-fathers, where he and his family set up home in Edinburgh. The following year he moved the mission's headquarters to Stirling, and the Blacks settled in nearby Callander.

Tony has now left the Leprosy Mission, and is in charge of the International Revival Network – which distributes revival news and information across the Internet. Solid links have been formed with revival leaders like John Arnott and Wes Campbell from Canada. 'Revivals have petered out in the past. I believe God wants this stream to keep flowing in at one end – and going out the other. If we'll be faithful in giving it out through mercy mission to the poor and giving the gospel to the poor, he will pour it in at one end. It will go on for as long as we're prepared to give it away.' Tony echoed the sentiment that John Arnott often promotes: 'to walk in God's love, and then give it away'.

Like his colleagues, Tony is concerned about moving out of renewal and into revival. 'I believe this Scottish nation, the British Isles, is going to be a great mission sending nation again,' he told delegates at 'Scotland Ablaze!' An important factor, he believes, will be mercy mission. As a practical out-working of that, people were encouraged to contribute to an offering. 'This isn't old-style mission,' said Tony. 'This is where the stream of renewal and revival will go – with the money and the missionaries.'

Another key theme was forgiveness. People reflected on reconciliation between the ancient tribes of the British Isles. John and Carol Arnott spoke about forgiveness on the Saturday night, and it just happened to be the eve of the day that would see the notorious Drumcree march get underway in Northern Ireland.

Encouraging husbands and wives to embrace and say 'sorry' to one another, John said, 'It's one of the greatest enemies of revival – the fact that we want justice for others but mercy for ourselves.' Couples could be seen hugging and making amends.

The following morning, Tony talked about the marching season in Ulster. Delegates from both the north and south of Ireland shared some insight and led the audience in prayer. On behalf of the conference, Tony thanked John Arnott for his timely message the night before. 'It applies to the whole of the British Isles,' he said. 'At the end of the day, we have to forgive.' He outlined some of the issues he had been thinking through, as a Scotsman with an English accent:

> There are two things an Englishman thinks about Scotland – that it's a beautiful nation, and that they're a warrior-like people. They get a shock when they come up here and find that not all of us always think kindly of them! Attitudes have to change. The flowing of revival from this nation to the ends of the earth will only come if we stop blaming the English. Unforgiveness is deathly. It's the same in Ireland and Wales. We've all got to get on with it. Apologies, new friendships and servant hearts are the key.

As he spoke, there were sounds of weeping among the audience. 'We've been hearing the word "freedom" over Scotland for a couple of years since the [*Braveheart*] movie,' he said. 'That was symbolic. It was prophetic. Now I believe the day has come. This is the day! This is the year!'

10 *Alternative Ulster*

'Sweet Music to Belfast's Ears' – so read the headline in *The Times* about a new £32 million concert hall for the city. Opened in January 1997, the Waterfront Hall is a bold response to the Troubles. Its glass dome and walls are in direct contrast to the solid fortifications that surround the courthouse just across the road. Its optimism stands out, there on the banks of the Lagan.

Some big names perform at the Waterfront, too – from pop to classical. A massive painting of George Best hangs over one of the stairwells. You can buy a cup of coffee there, and sit and gaze at the water's surface. But another river is flowing – a spiritual one that has been changing lives by the score. It struck the Waterfront one spring weekend.

The hall was half full with hyperactive, trendy teenagers. They had gathered for the 'Desert Festival', which effectively kicked off a whole weekend's celebration to mark the tenth anniversary of Christian Fellowship Church – or CFC, as it has become known. Ireland's second largest church, CFC is very much a charismatic renewal centre. And first on the evening's bill was – of all things – a former drug addict from Texas.

No longer high on illegal substances, Barry Bynum was now playing the blues for Jesus. Barry used to be lead guitarist for an American rock band called Liberation Suite. They had been one of the frontline ministries emerging from the 'Jesus Revolution' – a wave of lively, culturally relevant Christianity that swept across the States and found its way to the shores of the British Isles.

Lib Suite, as they became known, were different from the usual folk-rock groups that performed in church halls in the 1970s in an effort to convey 'contemporary' Christianity. They played loud, hard rock with a gritty guitar sound, 'bluesy' vocals, horns and synthesizers. They gave an 'in-your-face' gospel message at each concert. Many would respond to the call for commitment.

Before his own conversion, Barry had taken drugs since the age of 14. 'In Texas there was a lot available,' he said. 'We were close to Mexico and things were just growing in your backyard. So it was very cheap and accessible. And it was very popular at the time. The whole cannabis, hash and speed thing was very big, and loads of my friends were taking acid and stuff.' Thus the band emerged from that southern states drug scene:

> The funny thing is, when you're stoned you think you're really good – and the only people who think you're good are stoned too! It's like Dolby noise reduction. You record it in Dolby, and you've got to listen to it in Dolby. We were one of those bands who thought we were so special, we were the only ones who understood that we were this good. In other words we were horrible! We were playing gigs and never being invited back! We'd be playing songs 30 minutes long while the organizers were trying to throw us out the door.

Suddenly, the band members became Christians – all of them within the space of about six weeks. 'A whole troop of us came to the Lord, and God started dealing with us rapidly. Some of it was a bit of a blur. We were coming out of the drug thing. Things were happening fast.'

Whisked out of the drug culture, this bunch of young people became part of a network of house churches. Set free indeed, they called themselves Liberation Suite and played major Christian festivals – including Greenbelt in the UK. Their self-titled debut album was a landmark recording in Christian music. The band had broken up by 1991, but have kept in touch ever since. Yet Barry didn't feel he could abandon the adventure completely for an 'ordinary' American lifestyle.

'God started prompting something in our hearts. We'd done one short tour of Ireland in 1990. It sparked something in me, and made me feel there was more to do here. The British Isles had been very close to our hearts, but Ireland especially so. I felt God was saying, "You should go over there and watch what I'm going to do."' That was in 1993.

Barry and his wife Kristi moved to Belfast in what was really a step of faith financially. 'We got here and in the space of two or three months, things really took off. I became busy working at Christian events of all types – outreach projects, concerts, coffee bars, schools – those sort of things. And it has steadily got more and more busy. What we thought might be a year out has been four years.'

Another act lined up for Belfast's Desert Festival was a young man called Brian Houston. He has been regarded by many of his peers as the uncrowned king of the local music scene, and his recordings have sold well. His 1997 album, *Good News Junkie*, featured contributions from 10cc guitarist Graham Gouldman and Level 42's drummer Gary Husband.

He has played on the same bill as Van Morrison, Elvis Costello and Squeeze, yet Brian is still very much an untold story across the rest of these islands. Inspired as a youngster by Elvis Presley, he plays rootsy, robust rock 'n' roll, in the vein of Van Morrison and Bruce Springsteen. He led the worship at the Waterfront Hall celebrations. Brian also played in Kevin Prosch's band when the well-known worship leader and singer-songwriter visited Belfast in 1993:

It was the biggest thing that ever affected me. We did four or five gigs. And every night we played, I just cried. I knew from the first night that every bar of music I had played had been a waste of time prior to that moment – that my life had been totally self-centred, my music had been totally about me, and that I didn't even understand for a minute what it was about. And I began to see that it was about something really special and really powerful.

In 1996 Brian visited Toronto Airport Christian Fellowship, and heard a talk by veteran American rock singer Larry Norman – another leading light in the 'Jesus Revolution'. Larry warned against the dangers of watering down the truth in order to succeed and sell more records. Brian says: 'I can relate to that in the sense that I have adapted and changed and moulded and moved to try to make it in the music business. Now I'd rather adapt and change and mould and move more in the Jesus business. It probably sounds corny, but it's just about your life reflecting that. It's about serving him, about showing people the way.'

Brian thought he didn't have 'a huge compassion' for those who didn't know God. 'But when I get up on the stage and God's Spirit moves, I crack up crying.' His Canadian visit is reflected in one of his more recent songs, 'Orangeville', which adds a taste of revival to the *Junkie* album. It is about a place just outside Toronto where he was invited to lead worship. 'God moved and touched people so much in a powerful way,' he said. 'I wrote that song, and I've spoken to some people who weren't in Toronto but who heard it on the secular radio. And they've begun to be affected in the Toronto way – while driving along in the car! God's kind of funny that way.'

CFC's weekend of celebrations climaxed with their own presentation, 'Victory', on Pentecost Sunday. Using music, dance, drama and a sprinkling of comedy, the 'musical extravaganza' told the story of redemption through Jesus. In a burst of spectacular lights, colourful costumes and gospel music, a seeker-friendly, non-sectarian spirituality was portrayed – mostly by the church members themselves. Producer and director was Marie Lacey, herself an accomplished singer with an impressive voice. She is often described as Ireland's leading vocalist in the gospel/soul world, and is part of the worship team at CFC in Strandtown, Belfast.

'We live in a land where all sides of the community seek to conquer rather than be conquered,' she said. 'As this constant quest for "victory" over each other seems to be insatiable, it's time for the followers of Christ to declare that the victory of Jesus alone can release us from hatred, division and sectarianism.' Marie is part of this gold seam of highly talented artistes who have emerged from the CFC 'family'.

Senior Pastor of CFC is Paul Reid, a very tall and very friendly man. 'There's a lot of people looking at Ireland from all over the world,' he said. 'Ireland's hot at the moment – *Riverdance*, U2, the power of the Irish folklore and hospitality.' Paul has been in demand as a speaker at churches and conferences across these islands – particularly the whole 'cell church' concept, which CFC have adopted. Now 46, his formative years in the faith were spent within the Brethren denomination. It was at one such church that he met Priscilla, who later became his wife:

We taught Sunday school, did children's meetings and coffee bars. We were together for seven and a half years before we got married. A turning point in my life was 1979 when we went to the first ever Spring Harvest. Up to then we weren't open to the gifts of the Spirit. However, from then on we were hungry for more of God – but not hungry for tongues!

They started a little meeting where they were living at the time, at a village in Northern Ireland. 'No one was converted and we said, "God, what's wrong?" And the Lord said, "What would you do now if I saved six people?" I said we'd send them along to the Baptists! As I often say, taking an average teenager to our Brethren Assembly would be like taking your granny to a disco. So we just couldn't do it. Then we just began to say, "Lord, what have you got for us?"'

In 1981 they paid a return visit to Spring Harvest, and they felt God spoke to them on the last night through the ministry of controversial Bible teacher David Pawson. He spoke on Deuteronomy 1, and the message was, 'it's time to move from this mountain'. David said it was the first time he had ever made an appeal for people called to leadership. 'Three hundred went forward,' said Paul, 'and we were out there.'

Arriving back home, they realized God had called them to 'do something new'. They started a little group in Paul's half-brother's front room on 1 September 1981. There were just 11 adults – 'and the ladies had their heads covered with scarves,' said Paul. 'We learned something about community. That was probably the heart of what we were about.' Yet another trip to Spring Harvest was made in 1983, where Paul experienced the baptism of the Spirit – 'and that really wrecked things then'! He started to have visions and dreams. 'It was like a door opening to the supernatural for me,' he explained. 'A number of others came on board and said, "We're in with you, mate – pray for us." They got baptized in the Spirit and we just went from there. Someone lit a fire under me in a new way and I sort of went – whoosh!'

However, the whole thing was a struggle for his wife Priscilla. For 11 months she fought an inner battle. 'I was from a Brethren background,' she said. 'I had a great mum and dad who loved the Lord. So I was going through thoughts like, "Why hasn't my father experienced this?" That was a big stumbling block – until I got so desperate for God that he just broke through.'

One night she, too, asked for prayer – though nothing actually happened then:

I'd been prayed for a few times before that, and I was like schizophrenic. I kept thinking, 'I want something to happen.' But I was terrified in case something did! Then I felt the Lord saying to me, 'How did you receive your salvation?' By faith. Then he said, 'Well, now you are asking to be baptized in the Spirit, I want you to receive it by faith.' Now I could do that! So I said, 'Lord, I am receiving.' I didn't speak in tongues or anything like that. But a short time later I was feeding one of the kids, praying for a difficult situation – when suddenly I began to pray in tongues. I was so excited, the baby got milkshake that night!

Priscilla believes baptism in the Spirit revolutionized her worldview. 'It was mind blowing,' she said. 'I'd see things in Scripture that I'd never seen before. We used to joke about it. We'd say that someone had gone through our Bible and put verses in that hadn't been there before. It was a heady experience.' Priscilla now has a ministry in her own right. Alongside her storytelling work in the community, she's an elder in the church, runs their Alpha course and speaks across Ireland, the United Kingdom and the United States.

A general air of excitement was rising in the church, which by that stage consisted of about 25 people. 'Some were a bit nervous that we were turning it into a Pentecostal church,' said Paul. 'But what really blew it apart was our link-up with the discipleship movement.'

Numbers were added to the congregation, and Paul was invited to join the eldership in 1985. But their preoccupation with the controversial practice of 'shepherding' – a very close monitoring of each other's lives – proved to be their downfall. 'If God is for you and on your side,' said Paul, 'even if you do stupid things, God can still make you look good. But if God's against you, even if you have the slickest show in the world, it doesn't work. We had a lot of talent among us – but I think God was wanting to deal with something in us. No matter what we did, nothing went right.'

In 1986 the leaders called a special meeting – and resigned. 'We said we'd sinned over issues of control, self-righteousness and idolatry,' Paul explained, 'and men were given honour that should have been given to God. We basically said, "We've taken you down the wrong path." It was a hard time. I thought God would never use me again. We cried. We sobbed. We were broken.'

By now, Paul was working three days a week in his own wholesale business. He and his fellow leaders didn't know where to take the church from there; it was eventually decided that a vote would be taken for an interim leadership. 'We didn't stand,' said Paul, 'we said, we're beat.' But even so, later it seemed that God was calling him back into leadership.

In December 1986 they formed an eldership, and a new church began to rise from the ashes. Paul started working full time for the church in April 1987. 'In the third week of May I called the church together and said, "This is where we are going." That was really the beginning of this new phase.'

The mid-1990s were another milestone in the church's history, when renewal hit them in a deeper way. It was January 1994, and Paul received a phone call from a former elder of CFC who had emigrated to Toronto and joined what was then a little known Vineyard church on the edge of the airport. 'He said that an amazing thing happened with this guy called Randy Clark,' Paul remembered. 'They were praying for some kids and they all fell down. They kept the meetings going. Then of course the stories started coming out.'

That summer, Paul had a dream. 'I was in my pyjamas, carrying a little candle,' he said. 'I was in a hotel lobby and every single person in the church was there. I shone the light under their faces and said, "Do you want more of God?" They all said "Yes."' So all the signs were indicating that the Toronto experience was worth investigating, but initially Paul didn't really want to go:

> Priscilla said I should. One Sunday night I said if God shows me by tomorrow morning that I need to go, and somebody asks me, then I will go. I got up in the morning and there was a postcard from Toronto from a girl who'd been living in London for six years. I said, 'Lord, if you want me to go I need somebody to pay for me.' I was talking to a friend of mine from church and said, 'Do you fancy going?' He went out of the room and came back, and said, 'I can't go – but here's £500.'

By the end of August 1994, a 12-strong delegation was on its way to Toronto from CFC. 'On the first night I was sat in the meeting,' said Paul, 'and this man started to twitch. I put my Bible up so I wouldn't see him. As soon as I did that, I fell on the ground and laughed for 2 hours and 20 minutes. I had the most profound experience.'

An IRA ceasefire started while they were away on 1 September 1994. The Belfast group returned on a Saturday night. 'On the Sunday morning we had what I can only describe as a Pentecost,' said Paul. 'God came – and we were the centre of Toronto activity. We ran extra meetings. It was just unbelievable.'

Belfast gave a mixed reception to the Toronto experience. On the one hand there was great opposition from those who would not accept the gifts of the Spirit, yet on the other hand

the renewal broke down barriers between denominations –
as both Church of Ireland and Presbyterians became affected.
'So there was a great sense of unity,' said Paul. 'That really
helped us.'

The biggest challenge for any active church in Belfast, of
course, has been the Troubles. Unity and reconciliation are
brave words indeed – and CFC has a strong commitment
towards healing the hurts of Northern Ireland. Paul says:

> Every generation has two words from God – the timeless
> word of the gospel – and the 'now' word which is applic-
> able to their situation. To William Carey it was overseas
> mission. For us, we need to address the whole issue of rec-
> onciliation. Possibly the biggest thing for us is the division
> in the body of Christ over here. People have failed to
> recognize that there are other people who don't share their
> exact beliefs but genuinely love Jesus Christ.

CFC has adopted its own emphasis. It promotes the idea
that becoming a Christian doesn't mean you don't become a
Protestant or Catholic. 'The Gentiles didn't have to become
Jews to come into the body of Christ,' said Paul. 'In our con-
text, that means Catholics don't have to become Protestants.
It's not that the Jews stayed Jews and the Gentiles stayed
Gentiles. The two became one. There needs to be a visible
expression of the two becoming one.'

At CFC, people keep their political aspirations and cultural
identity. 'But we are one in Christ – and we meet together
and celebrate that,' said Paul. He recognizes that there are
Catholics who are Christians, and there are Christians who
are Protestants. 'But we don't want to be called either,' he
said, 'we are neither.'

The church is a spiritual home for those with nationalist
aspirations and nationalist culture, as well as for those with

unionist aspirations and unionist culture. Former paramilitaries from both sides, people who have lost loved ones in the conflict, and officers of the Royal Ulster Constabulary, all have worshipped there.

'In terms of the body of Christ,' said Priscilla, 'we are one family. We feel passionately about that.' Sadly, she pointed out, the wider Church in Northern Ireland has been 'a major part of the problem'. Paul added that people from a Catholic background can feel very intimidated when they go into a Protestant church adorned with union jacks, emblems, symbols, and memorials to the wars. 'One guy said CFC was the only church he could find where he didn't have to surrender his nationalist identity and culture and become a Protestant,' explained Paul. 'There are other similar stories. We have a very definite stand on that.'

CFC has been forging links with the Catholic community, and its members meet with a charismatic Catholic group called Lamb of God. 'We feel God has done something special in our relationship,' said Paul. 'They're still committed Catholics. I think the difficulty in unity is that you try to pretend you are more united than you really are. That's a mistake. We admit we have differences. What unites us is life in Jesus Christ. We're prepared to stand together, witness together and worship and pray.'

Paul works with other groups, too, in a bid to promote peace. Among those he has been meeting with is Sinn Fein – before they were even admitted into the official peace process. 'I met with them on a monthly basis in a secret location,' he said. Paul believes it gave him a better understanding of both sides of the argument:

The two priests who brokered the IRA ceasefire with the British government – Father Al Reid and Gerry Reynolds – got a group of Christians together. We began to meet with members of Sinn Fein to try and understand and hear each other. Out of that formed a lot of contacts. We've also had quite a few one-day conferences where we bring a wider group of people together. It's all about listening to each other, to hear what the other people are saying. We had some stormy meetings and honest conversations – especially after atrocities.

Belfast is a larger-than-life city, with some of the most impressive historic buildings in the British Isles. There are signs of prosperity and growth, and much money has been spent on developing parts of the locality, like the riverside projects – of which the Waterfront Hall has been a part. But there are areas of Belfast where 'impoverished' is an understatement. CFC is working there, too. 'We have quite a major social community impact which is a ministry to the poor and needy,' said Paul. 'We have a house in the inner city given to us by the council. We run a project for those who can't get on to training courses for jobs.'

To date, the CFC family of churches includes the parent congregation in Strandtown, a district of Belfast, with other groups meeting in Holywood, Carrickfergus, Cregah, Bangor, Newtownards, Lisburn, Dublin and Downpatrick – a mixture of urban and rural communities. In total, the network has well over 2,000 members.

To cover the areas effectively, CFC has invested whole-heartedly in the 'cell church' movement. The emphasis is taken off the big meeting and put on the small group or cell. Belfast is a series of villages all linked together; and CFC is following a vision for a large city church that breaks down into areas and cells.

In a place where even the evangelical community suffers from division and sectarianism, unity 'has to be in the heart', said Paul, 'you have to work it out'. He added, 'If you as a church are not tackling and grappling with the problem, what's the relevance of the gospel to society?'

There have been sporadic revivals in Ireland's history. In Ulster in 1859, 100,000 people became Christians in one year. The charismatic movement of the 1970s led to a massive boom in prayer groups across Catholic parishes in the south. But as a whole, Ireland has not seen an awakening like the kind that happened through the ministry of St Patrick.

Romano-Briton by origin, Patrick and his companions established the Christian Church throughout Ireland on lasting foundations. He travelled throughout the country preaching, teaching, building churches, opening schools and monasteries, converting chiefs and bards. He has been called the 'Apostle of Ireland'. Whether it's fact or symbolism, he is said to have driven out snakes from the country. 'Fifteen hundred years ago there was a revival which affected the darkness of western Europe,' said Paul. 'We're praying for revival which will span the churches – and touch the nations again.'

11 *Seeds of revival*

'Church takes mission to supermarket aisles'; 'Disgraced clergyman asks for forgiveness'; 'Charismatics offer secret prayers for Blair'. Those were among the major headlines in *The Times* on the very morning I sat down to finalize the contents of this book. The impression given was of a Church reaching out in fresh ways to a new post-Christian generation; a Church attempting to deal with its own internal problems; and a Church interfacing with the crucial issues of our day.

Later that same evening, BBC2's *Newsnight* covered the 'Diana prophecy' that reportedly boosted people's hopes for a spiritual awakening. Seasoned BBC newsman Ted Harrison – a likeable man who has covered various religious stories over the year – presented a balanced report of this unusual message. Baptist Church member Ginny Burgin claimed to have received a word from God some months before the actual death of Princess Diana. The prophecy pointed quite specifically to a time of national mourning with flowers being placed in cities.

News spread like wildfire. Thousands of copies of the message were distributed across many churches of different networks and denominations. The *Newsnight* report particularly focused on regular revival meetings spearheaded by New Church leader Gerald Coates at the Emmanuel Centre, Westminster. A visitor had shown Gerald a copy of the prophecy, and he checked out its source before distributing it among his own contacts. Even the mere expectation of revival can now make the news.

When mourners camped out on the streets of London to watch Diana's funeral cortège, a much smaller stream of people converged on the Emmanuel Centre for one of the revival meetings. It was a quiet gathering. And while the faithful met for prayer at what has become known as 'the Marsham Street meetings', scores of passers-by quietly drifted in off the streets to sign a book of condolences that was set out on a table in the lobby.

Gerald Coates gave the official welcome at the front of the main hall. Arguably one of the more controversial leaders in the charismatic movement, Gerald leads the Pioneer network of 'New Churches'. He pointed out how the death of Diana had already been likened to that of President Kennedy. It was said that Kennedy's assassination left a big spiritual void in America; and that soon after, the 'Jesus Movement' exploded on the scene. At that time, leading figures from the music scene and showbusiness world started declaring their new-found Christian faith. A thriving subculture of youth rallies, 'gospel rock' concerts and Christian filmshows developed. Could a similar thing be happening in Britain, triggered by Diana's death, Gerald suggested?

'Pray for our nation at such a time as this,' he told the Marsham Street crowd. 'Dare we believe that some great spiritual movement that could turn the nation around could come out of this? Let's pray God will do some great thing.' Then he spoke of the shocking irony of Mother Teresa's death. It was obvious from the stunned faces around the auditorium that some people had not heard the news. The effect was immediate. People were encouraged to fill the Emmanuel Centre with prayer – and to remember the Royal Family and the Al Fayeds. It felt like a significant moment.

Gerald handed the meeting over to his friend and colleague Martin Scott to lead the intercession. 'We're here to dig a well for our nation,' said Martin, a thin, friendly man from the Orkneys. 'There are so many people out on the streets, literally sheep without a shepherd. Let's begin to open up our hearts, that this night has a purpose.'

Voices rose. People prayed that God would come. 'We ask that this be a season of visitation,' Martin cried, stalking around at the front of the hall like a hunter. Behind him a big, bright banner bore the simple motif in striking lettering: revival. Though modest in comparison to world renewal centres like Toronto or Pensacola, the long-running series of meetings at Marsham Street, Westminster, has still attracted much media interest, according to Pioneer's *Compass* magazine, of which Gerald is senior editor.

Called 'Sowing the Seeds of Revival', the events had by that stage drawn more than 60,000 people since they first started in the summer. About 7,000 had so far responded to the call to 'get right with God'. Press coverage had been widespread – with stories appearing in the *Independent on Sunday*, *The Sunday Times*, the *Observer*, various London newspapers, and daily papers in Spain, Australia, Japan and the Netherlands. Radio 4, Radio 5, BBC2's *Newsnight* and Germany's RTL television have also run features. 'The Marsham Street meetings have received a level of attention out of all proportion to their size,' said Gerald, 'and I believe that's due to a change of mood across the country – particularly in this post-Diana age.' Testimonies have been circulated from 'Seeds of Revival':

Susan had been brought along to the Marsham Street meetings by a friend. She explained that she was born a heroin addict, was recently drunk and on drugs, and engaged in the sort of behaviour that goes with that lifestyle. 'She looked absolutely terrible,' one of the leaders explained. Susan received prayer on several occasions. One evening while personal prayer ministry was going on, Gerald went for a 'walkabout' around the meeting. He stopped to ask one of the intercessors a question and she pointed to her left. Aware that Coates was confused by the gesture, she said, 'It's Susan.' Coates said he was 'absolutely astonished'. She was barely recognizable from the woman who'd been in the meeting a few weeks previously. Susan hadn't had a drink in a month – and had come off drugs. 'It was almost unbelievable,' added Gerald.

There are many other similar stories of remarkable life changes as a result of people attending the Westminster meetings:

Chris is a 22-year-old man who four years previously had bought a pornographic magazine. By July 1997 he'd accumulated four large boxes full of pornographic videos and magazines. They were worth several thousands of pounds. One night, having been to Marsham Street on several occasions, he was so deeply convicted with his sin, he brought the boxes along to a meeting. Interviewed sometime later, Chris explained, 'I couldn't get rid of them privately. I'd sinned in private for four years – I had to repent in public.'

Peter leads a church of several hundred at a town in Surrey. 'After Marsham Street will I ever be the same again?' he wrote. Asked in one of the meetings what getting right with God meant to him, he replied, 'I have found faith again.' The effects were seen in scores repenting quite publicly to appeals at his own church over the following weeks.

There have been bizarre manifestations, too. One young man visited Marsham Street one night and was prayed for.

Throughout the latter part of the evening, he turned to friends and kept saying, 'I feel like I'm on fire.' Eventually as a group they left for McDonald's. Yet still he continued saying, 'I feel as though I'm on fire.' Suddenly the fire alarms went off. When the fire brigade arrived, they found no fire. The man quipped, 'You can't put the fires of revival out.'

Other attention has been negative. Gerald and his team have learned that there is a price to pay when you make a stand for revival. Severe criticism has been levelled at Gerald and the Marsham Street initiative. Accusations were actually published in a booklet called *An Open Invitation to Gerald Coates from a Pentecostal Preacher* – which had unauthorized distribution outside the Westminster meetings as people went in.

In the summer 1998 edition of Pioneer's *Compass* magazine, Gerald responded to some of the most frequently asked questions about revival. In the light of his message that 'revival is here, and is on its way', where were the huge numbers being saved? And why did he embrace a prophetic prediction that the greatest revival would hit Britain in October 1990? To the first question, he gave this reply:

> Let's be clear. Britain is not in full blown revival. I don't know anyone who's saying that. But around 4,000 prisoners have made public confessions of faith in recent years. Some 16–20,000 gypsies have done the same. Around 500,000 have or are going through Alpha, a course which explains the gospel. An acquaintance of mine leads a church which has grown from 400 to 4,000 in less than ten years. And schools workers up and down the country tell me of a far greater openness amongst teachers and children to the gospel. Those are well documented facts. And we pray it is but a fresh wave of the gospel affecting every area of our culture.

In responding to the second challenge about the revival prophecy, Gerald claimed he didn't know what was prophesied, who prophesied it, or where it was prophesied. He said he was not present when any such prophecy was given. He hadn't seen it in print. He hadn't even heard it on tape. 'Neither was I present at the meetings, which I believe were in Docklands East London, when all of this was supposed to have taken place,' he added.

However, we have to admit it is a challenge that there are so many evangelicals – including charismatic evangelicals – and yet the country is still in a bad state. It's up to each of us as individuals, local churches and networks to make Christ attractive and intelligible to those around us. Without a massive outpouring of the Holy Spirit, I don't know what's going to happen to our children and our children's children. We should take note of the challenge and ask for God's help to ensure we are looking up and out to the society around us. Personally I'm asking God to help me live for Christ, expressed in revival, relationships and relevance.

It seems that even the most venomous critic may find it hard to bring the kiss of death to the revival ministry pioneered at Marsham Street. 'In the Azuza Street revival at the beginning of this century,' said Gerald, 'many of the people who became Christians didn't attend the meetings because of any great spiritual hunger – but because they were inquisitive about all the controversy.'

12 *Beyond the 'Blessing'*

Nearly 1,000 people were packed into the huge sports dome near the Busch Gardens theme park, Florida. But they hadn't come to cheer at a game, although there was plenty of shouting going on. Some even showed signs of drunkenness as they staggered around throughout the morning. By the afternoon, most of the 950 people were laid out on the floor. They had come to The River at Tampa Bay – the church founded by controversial revivalist Rodney Howard-Browne.

It is unusual in that it is a church born out of an established revival ministry. Normally, such organizations start off in churches – not the other way round. And it is headed by a man not usually associated with pastoral issues. At the time of our interview in spring 1998, the church was barely 15 months old – 'a baby church' as Rodney calls it – yet with 1,100 members; and already there were plans to use an even bigger arena.

Rodney also runs a Bible school nearby. At that time they had 340 students from 36 states and 12 foreign countries enrolled for a one-year course. On top of all that, Rodney travels all over the world preaching – and urging people to 'have another drink'. It sounds a gruelling schedule – it's a miracle that he manages to fit it all in:

> We travel in the crusades every week. So we fly out on Tuesday, fly back Saturday. I've not missed one Sunday since we started the church. If I go to Africa I jump on the plane on the Sunday afternoon – like now I would be on a plane flying out – and I get in there within an hour or

two for the meeting, have to run on the platform and I preach till Thursday, jump on the plane, and I'm back in Miami early hours of Saturday morning. If I come to the UK I'll do the same, I jump on a plane on the Sunday evening, get there on Monday, stay Monday through to Thursday or Friday – and then fly back Saturday. That's what we're doing.

Rodney shows commitment to the concept of local church; that's because he believes he is modelling something. 'This is what the Lord told us to do,' he said, 'yet everyone says you can't have revival in the local church. That's what they say: "It's going to ruin your church." But we feel you can.'

That particular Sunday at The River, every element of Rodney's revival meetings was there – such as spontaneous joy, prayer for healing and extended times of worship. 'But there was a pastoral message on boldness,' he said. 'We feel you can have revival. But you can't have it in an hour and a half. You know what I'm saying? You can't have it in two hours. You've just got to leave the Lord free to work.'

Rodney was raised in a Pentecostal home in South Africa. At the age of five he made a Christian commitment. Three years later he had an experience of being 'filled with the Holy Spirit'.

Both at home and at church he saw supernatural manifestations while he was growing up. His parents would listen to sermons by the famous healing evangelist Kathryn Kuhlman on their reel-to-reel tape recorder. Sometimes they would pray from seven in the evening until two in the morning. Yet even though he was brought up in such a spiritually charged environment, Rodney craved for more. He was hungry for God. He then discovered 'the anointing':

. . . when the Lord touched me in 1979 I was 18 years old. The fire fell on me for three and a half days. In 1980 I went into the ministry, worked for Youth for Christ, travelled in southern Africa, got married in '81 and just carried on travelling. When the power of God hit me in '79 I was so drunk and beside myself, and filled with joy, I was laughing, crying . . . what we see happening in the meetings – that's what happened to me in '79. I just didn't know what to do with it.

Experiencing the power of God for himself was a key turning point. From 1980 onwards Rodney embarked on a powerful revival ministry. During a run of successful meetings in New York state in 1989, people said they saw a cloud come down and fill the room. Many fell out of their seats. Rodney said it was as if someone was shooting them! Later he preached back in his homeland of South Africa:

Over 100,000 people got touched. We were in the city of Pinetown, just outside of Durban. The revival ran for four weeks. That was the first extended revival we'd had. That was in August of 1990. It was a four-week revival. Then we moved into Durban and we actually stayed seven and a half weeks. We went from a 1,400-seater to a 2,500-seater to a 5,000 seater. That was the progression. Then the Lord said to me, 'I've done it in your home country, I'm going to do it in America.' We came back here. It hit Alaska, North Dakota, and '92 was the east coast of Florida, and '93 was central Florida. Then it just went 'ka-boom'. It was like a bomb went off. I met Randy Clark in January of '94, in Lakeland.

Rodney's forthright manner and blunt honesty may have distanced some rather more conservative Christians from him. Some have disliked his friendships with those from the so-called 'prosperity' camp. But Rodney doesn't preach about a God who gives out free Cadillacs to anyone who asks.

What he does preach is that anyone can receive God's abundant power if they crave for it:

> It's been the greatest adventure of our lives. The last nine years have been incredible. I wouldn't swap it for anything in the world – seeing people saved, healed, set free, delivered, on fire, ministers back into the ministry, churches doubling, trebling, quadrupling. I mean, you always hear about the churches that lost people. But churches lose people because they didn't have revival! It's awesome. And I'm so happy, so excited. I'm beside myself with joy.

His enthusiasm is infectious. And though his critics would beg to differ, it is hard not to like this big South African, with his humorous preaching style and generous use of illustrations. When you meet him face to face, his humility shines through. Interestingly, some of his own ancestors were from Wales, the country of revival.

As he travels around the world, Rodney sees much that encourages him. In his view, the revival scene is 'as hot as it's ever been'. He found that in the early days of his ministry, people would come along just to look. 'Now they've made the decision, and now you've got hungry people. And it's awesome. It's much greater than it was in '93, '94, '95. It's wonderful.' Others would claim the manifestations have died down, and perhaps that was just a phase or 'season' that churches were going through. So what's Rodney's response to that?

> What are they talking about? . . . I tell you what, a lot of people stop getting hungry for God and what happens is they say, 'Well, we've been here, we've seen that, we've done that.' You have to be like a child. You have to just come open to God and hungry. The children of Israel were like that – 'this manna again' – that kind of stuff. We have

to be careful with that. God's not stopped. He's still moving. He's still touching people.

People have said of Rodney and others like him that what they are promoting is renewal, not revival. But he disagrees. Rodney feels their concept of revival is about getting people converted. 'But I say this – if you get people saved, you bring them into what? You bring them into a dead church.' However, if church people experience the power of God in their lives, that makes them into soul-winners. 'If the fire of God is on you, the automatic thing that's going to happen is that you're going to be out there winning people for Jesus – everywhere you go.' So what is the big goal that he's aiming for?

Well, we're pushing for global revival – global awakening – the Great Awakening. The seeds are being sown. You can't go any place in the world and not find people that have been touched in some way, shape or fashion by the current wave. But this is only the beginning. This is only the very start of what God wants to do. The greatest harvest of souls is going to come in, that's going to make the Day of Pentecost look like a Sunday school picnic. My dream is to see cities like London, New York, and some of the major cities hit with such a wave of God. I'm not talking about one church. We've seen local church revivals. I'm talking about city-wide where there are traffic jams. It's a dream I have – where nightclubs close down, where bars close down, where abortion clinics close down, where university campuses have to be closed for three, four, five days at a time because no one can function. The power of God just hits the whole place. That's what I live with. I know some people say, 'Well, that's impossible, it's never going to happen.' I believe just like when Jonah went to Nineveh, the place repented, God's going to give us some cities. We're going to see whole cities shaken to their very core.

That's what Rodney says he's believing God for. 'We've seen local revivals in local churches,' he pointed out, 'but this next thing God is about to do is much bigger.'

13 *Revival people*

St Patrick's Grave. A huge rock marks the spot. It may not be the great saint's precise burial place, but evidence points to his bones being interned somewhere in the grounds of Down Cathedral, at the Ulster town of Downpatrick in Northern Ireland. The remains of St Columba and St Brigid are also believed to have been moved to that same location, making it literally the final epic gathering of those titans of Celtic Christianity.

Downpatrick grew from a settlement at the entrance of Strangford Lough, where Patrick is said to have waded ashore in the year 432. He formed alliances with the local chieftain and soon converted him to Christianity – a process that was to be repeated throughout Ireland. It was from that area that Celtic monks went on to spread Christianity throughout Europe.

I made my own pilgrimage to the gravestone, accompanied by John Keating, a close friend and an Irishman. Both of us have been inspired by the story of Patrick. Both of us have desired a similar gifting and anointing. Both of us have a deep concern for the people of Ireland. As we reflected on the 'apostle of Ireland' by his graveside, John prayed that we would somehow be given the same mantle that God placed on Patrick.

According to Irish-American writer Thomas Cahill, Patrick, a Romano-Briton, won Ireland over to Christ by abandoning his own national roots. He effectively 'became' Irish, Cahill says in his book called *How the Irish Saved Civilization*. Patrick identified completely with the people group he sought to reach. He behaved like one of them, and in his own writings he even expressed himself as an Irishman.

That must be a lesson for those of us who want to become 'revival people', and help usher in a new spiritual awakening across these lands. A major key must be to relate totally to those around us who need a revelation of Christ. In the same way that Patrick related so closely that he even called himself Irish, dare *we* associate with our 'tribes' and communities at such a level that we assume their cultural and social ways?

'You left Ireland too early,' had been John Keating's cryptic comment to me a week before our visit to St Patrick's Grave. At that moment I had just returned home with my family from a spring half-term holiday in Belfast. We had stayed with our friends Jack Moore, minister of Bloomfield Road Methodist Church, and his wife, Liz. We had done the 'tourist things' – visiting Belfast Zoo and the Ulster Folk and Transport Museum. Now John was urging me to fly back to Belfast. Why? Because a four-day conference he had been leading had turned into a continuous series of revival-style meetings.

I was still in a bit of a daze from our ferry crossing and the long drive home, but within a few days I was taking my seat on a little plane at Gatwick Airport – returning to Northern Ireland. I felt as if I was doing totally the wrong thing – my children thought I was daft, too.

But from the moment I was met at Belfast City Airport, I knew this was to be a special weekend. That same evening I was driven to a sports hall, part of the complex of buildings at Hillsborough Elim Pentecostal Church, nestled amid some of the greenest hills I have ever seen. It is a beautiful setting.

The church was hosting the meetings, called 'Fireland'. What started as a weekend event had grown into a rolling programme of dynamic times of prayer and worship, sandwiched between the referendum on the Good Friday Peace

Agreement and the elections for the new Northern Ireland Assembly. Initially the meetings were extended by three days, then another three – almost repeating the same pattern as those first days of renewal in an insignificant building at the end of a runway in Toronto airport.

Finally, after the tenth night at Hillsborough – with expectancy and anticipation still running high – conference organizers and church leaders made the decision to carry on for another two weeks. The feeling among some was that the revival fervour could continue – *if* people wanted it enough. 'We have a window of opportunity,' John Keating told one of the meetings. 'What do you want?' 'Revival!' the crowd shouted back.

Fiery preaching targeted a few 'sacred cows' – such as religious tradition, the rule of men and the role of women in Ulster's church culture. Prophetic utterances like 'This is God's hour for Northern Ireland' almost brought the house down.

Loud drumming – a significant sound for Ulster – was used to enrich the atmosphere of praise. In this setting, though, it came across not as a sound of division, but a sound of spiritual freedom for people of all denominations or none. Music was certainly a key feature of the event, with times of worship running quite late into the evening programme. Few people seemed to mind.

With all the associated phenomena like laughter, shaking and falling over, Fireland could have been mistaken for Ulster's very own 'Toronto'. But as one couple remarked, 'We've had the refreshing. *This* is different.'

The week that Fireland started, at the end of May 1998, the *Belfast Telegraph* ran the headline: 'Shock Rise in Young Suicides'. A survey by the Samaritans had revealed how suicides had increased dramatically in Northern Ireland since the start of the year, and yet it was those very people who were responding to the appeals.

People suffering from severe depression became targets for prayer at the conference – with some remarkable results. Describing how one woman received healing at a meeting, team member Greg Austin said, 'You could *feel* the depression on her. She had attempted suicide on several occasions.' After he prayed with her, the woman fell to the floor, laughing uncontrollably and displaying symptoms of drunkenness. 'Three nights later, a woman showed up and stared right at me,' said Greg. 'Suddenly I realized it was the same person. The transformation on her countenance was incredible.' There were other similar stories supporting the team's conviction that God is healing the hurt of the last 30 years of sectarian conflict in Ulster.

Civil servant Colin McMinn also believed despair was being tackled at the meetings. 'We have a high incidence of post-traumatic depression as a result of the Troubles,' he said. 'But people show up at meetings like this – and suddenly they're just hit with the power of God. Their closed faces begin to open up and shine with the glory of Jesus.'

Fits of laughter came upon people wherever they stood at the Fireland meetings. That included those queuing up to put their cash gifts in the 'offering bucket'. People were dropping from their places in the line and rolling about on the floor laughing uncontrollably. It was the first time I have actually seen 'hilarious giving'!

Revival people will be infected with real joy so that their charitable giving will accelerate. At a purely practical level, they will see their donations as investments in a spiritual awakening, funding the workers and resources needed to spread the gospel. At a spiritual level, some believe the impartation of God's anointing is linked to giving. So as people become truly set free in the spiritual sense, one of the ways that that new freedom expresses itself is in a new generous attitude. Brian Agnew, at that time an elder at Hillsborough Elim, teaches on biblical economics and the

ministry of management. He believes two main keys to
revival are 'paying and praying'. As Brian simply put it,
'Labourers cost money.' Revival people will be committed to
those principles.

A growing number of people believe Ireland is significant
in God's plan for these islands – just as it was in Patrick's
day. As Geraldine Hogg put it, 'There's an expectancy and
anticipation that something is going to happen in Ireland.'
She and husband Terry are pioneering a fledgling 'church'
in a fiercely nationalist community of Ulster. They promote
a transcultural Christianity in a region where the labels
'Catholic' and 'Protestant' often have life-and-death conno-
tations. Yet Geraldine is convinced that a sweeping change
is on the horizon. 'I know it's going to take place – and it's
bigger than we've imagined because God is going to bring
something out of it. It's as if the very stones are crying out.'

Revival people will read the signs of the times. They will
be sensitive to the slightest breeze of God's Spirit. They will
spot the smallest signal of some spiritual need or happening
on the horizon. They will take serious note of prophetic
utterances, and they will respond with prayer and action.
Jesus rebuked the Pharisees for failing to see the signs. Few
Christians today would want to receive a similar charge.

Reconciliation is a big concern for Christians working in
Ireland, both north and south of the border. It has also been
on the hearts and minds of visiting Argentineans. Ed Silvoso
is founder and president of Harvest Evangelism, a mission
devoted to 'prayer evangelism'. On a visit to Britain in the
summer of 1998, he formally apologized on behalf of his
people for their country's part in the Falklands War.

'As unfortunate as the Falklands War was – and I want to
take a minute to apologize for that on our part – God used
that as an instrument of righteousness,' he told a packed
sports hall in Littlehampton, West Sussex. Ed explained that
the conflict toppled a cruel dictatorship, opening the door to
democracy, freedom – and revival. 'The revival broke out in

Argentina in full force, the night that the *General Belgrano* was sunk in a violent act of war,' he said. 'Now we have revival sweeping the land. And we have covenanted one million hours of prayer for revival to hit the United Kingdom.'

Ed had been in the United Kingdom for two weeks, speaking at major meetings in Portsmouth and the London borough of Haringey. 'We came at the worst possible time,' he said, 'the day Argentina and England played in the World Cup! But none of that was an obstacle. The English people are so gracious. The reception has been superb.' Accompanying them was a Falklands veteran called Herman, who had also come to ask forgiveness for the war. On a previous visit to the United Kingdom, Ed had met a sailor who'd been assigned to HMS *Sheffield*, the British destroyer sunk by Argentinian Exocet missiles. 'It was such a healing experience for both of us,' Ed said of their meeting. 'We see England as an instrument of righteousness, because through the war the dictatorship was brought down, and the revival kicked in. What the devil intended for evil, God was using for good. The devil tried to divide our nations. But, if anything, we're more united than ever in prayer and intercession.'

Revival people will put repentance and reconciliation high on their list of priorities. Already, new unity is coming about between the English and other such people groups as the Irish and Argentinians. If God was in the crucified Christ, reconciling the world to himself, he is also now in his people, reconciling them to one another.

I was approached by one German-speaking student in the beautiful grounds of Glendalough in southern Ireland. Our different cultures had previously been shaken by bitter division, but now we were about to be united in deep conversation amid this ancient monastic city in the Republic of Ireland. It is reputed to be a 'holy place' – visitors have reported a 'blanket of prayer' descending on them as they wander among the prayer cells, churches, round tower and Celtic crosses of the picturesque valley.

While reading the information boards in the visitor centre, I was asked by the young man, 'Excuse me, but what are "monks"?' It was an open invitation to talk about the gospel. I gave him the whole story of how the Christian message was spread across Europe during the Age of the Saints, and of how those fearless evangelists braved treacherous oceans in the process. Visibly impressed, he agreed there must be something in it – particularly as we were standing amid the evidence!

Revival people will find encouragement and inspiration from the stories of their forefathers of faith on these islands. According to Saint Arsenios of Cappadocia, 'When the Church in the British Isles begins to venerate her own saints, the Church will grow.' The dry bones, rusty relics and faded manuscripts of holy men and women from past generations still have much to tell us. What deep level of divine power did they encounter that compelled them to leave the comforts of home, set sail on fierce seas and let the wind of the Spirit blow them to distant pagan shores where they set up strategic mission bases to evangelize Britain and beyond?

My visit to St Patrick's Grave was followed by lunch in an Irish pub called Brendan's Bar – named, of course, after the saintly traveller who may well have been the first person to discover America. There is a small painting of him in his boat, just above the door into the lounge bar. The significance? Well, Patrick evangelized Ireland, and Brendan launched out from that dramatic coastline on what was also a voyage of spiritual discovery.

Revival people are on a journey. They pray for the spiritual climate to change, but they don't wait for the clouds to break. They embark on a 'Brendan voyage' to discover new adventures, new territories – as well as new dangers. They know revival is not just an event that may happen tomorrow. It is a process that can start today.